DEVELOPING
PROTOTYPIC
MEASURES OF
CROSS-CULTURAL
PRAGMATICS

DEVELOPING PROTOTYPIC MEASURES OF CROSS-CULTURAL PRAGMATICS

THOM HUDSON

EMILY DETMER

J. D. BROWN

SECOND LANGUAGE TEACHING & CURRICULUM CENTER
University of Hawai'i at Mānoa

Funds for the publication of this technical report were provided in part by a grant to the University of Hawai'i under the Language Resource Centers Program of the U. S. Department of Education.

ISBN 0–8248–1763–X

∞™ The paper used in this publication meets the minimum requirements of American National Standard for Information Sciences–Permanence of Paper for Printed Library Materials.

ANSI Z39.48–1984

Distributed by
University of Hawai'i Press
Order Department
2840 Kolowalu Street
Honolulu, Hawai'i 96822

ABOUT THE NATIONAL FOREIGN LANGUAGE RESOURCE CENTER

THE NATIONAL FOREIGN LANGUAGE RESOURCE CENTER (NFLRC) at the University of Hawai'i is funded by the U.S. Department of Education under a program that awards grants to a small number of institutions of higher education for the purpose of improving the nation's capacity to teach and learn foreign languages effectively. The NFLRC is housed in the Second Language Teaching and Curriculum Center, a unit of the College of Languages, Linguistics, and Literature. Under the general direction of a national advisory board and a local steering committee, the NFLRC conducts research, develops materials, and trains language professionals. A Fellows Program brings major scholars in foreign language acquisition to the University. A Summer Institute is held each year, at which teachers, teacher trainers, and program administrators can enhance their knowledge of current theory and practice in language pedagogy. The NFLRC publishes a series of Technical Reports (this volume is No. 7 in the series), research notes, and teaching materials. For more information about NFLRC programs, write:

Dr. Richard Schmidt, Director
National Foreign Language Resource Center
East-West Road, Bldg. 1, Rm. 6A
University of Hawai'i
Honolulu, HI 96822

NFLRC ADVISORY BOARD

Kathleen Bardovi-Harlig
Center for English Language Teaching
Indiana University

John Clark
Defense Language Institute
Monterey, California

Claire Kramsch
German Department
University of California, Berkeley

James Pusack
Project forInternational
Communication Studies (PICS)
University of Iowa

Ronald Walton
National Foreign Language Center
Johns Hopkins University

CONTENTS

APPENDICES

INTRODUCTION

FOR AT LEAST THE PAST DECADE, most models that have been developed to explain communicative language proficiency have included such independent yet related components as linguistic, sociolinguistic, pragmatic, and strategic competencies (Canale and Swain, 1980; Bachman, 1990). During that same period, the study of cross-cultural pragmatics has become an increasingly important area of applied linguistics (Kasper and Dahl, 1991; Blum-Kulka, 1982, 1987a, 1987b). This convergence of interest in such areas as the illocutionary and sociolinguistic competence of learners acquiring an additional language has encouraged language testing researchers to extend approaches to language testing (Canale and Swain, 1980; Bachman and Palmer, 1982; Canale, 1988; Bachman, 1990). As a result of the increasing interest in the study of pragmatics, a concomitant interest in developing appropriate and valid means for assessing such competence has emerged, although the development of procedures and instruments for systematically assessing cross-cultural pragmatics has not been widely addressed in measurement of language proficiency. While there are existing methods for assessing such areas of language competence as syntax, vocabulary, and cohesion, no generally accepted measures or methods for assessing the other components of communicative ability exist (Bachman, 1990).

One of the primary issues in developing instruments that assess cross-cultural pragmatic competence is associated with the variability of speaker behavior in discourse. The study of pragmatic ability inherently involves addressing two contributors to variability in performance: 1) variability associated with the social properties of the speech event, and the speaker's strategic, actional, and linguistic choices for achieving communicative goals;

Hudson, T., Detmer, E., & Brown, J. D. (1995). *Developing Prototypic Measures of Cross-Cultural Pragmatics* (Technical Report #7). Honolulu, Hawai'i: University of Hawai'i, Second Language Teaching & Curriculum Center.

and 2) variability due to the particular types of data collection procedures and associated instruments (Kasper and Dahl, 1991).

The present paper presents a description of phase two of a project that has attempted to develop instruments representing multiple methods for assessing cross-cultural pragmatics. The instruments that have been developed here are designed to provide information about both of the sources of variability mentioned in the previous paragraph. The paper discusses the quantitative and qualitative approaches that were applied in the development of prototypic instruments that may now be evaluated through administration to much larger cohorts of subjects. First, this paper briefly reviews the first phase of the project (Hudson, Detmer, and Brown, 1992). It then presents a detailed description of the instrument development process. It is hoped that a review of the development process will provide useful information for test users as well as provide future test developers with insights into the steps involved.

A BRIEF REVIEW OF PHASE ONE

THE FIRST PHASE OF THIS PROJECT (Hudson, Detmer, and Brown, 1992) involved first identifying the nature of the instruments and then determining the variables to be examined. These were iterative processes involving literature reviews and pilot testing of the instruments on small samples.

The process of identifying classifications of test types resulted in the three test types of: 1) indirect measures; 2) semi-direct measures; and 3) self-assessment measures. Additionally, each type of measure involved two test formats that vary along a scale of cued or free examinee response. The indirect measures that were identified for use were a free response discourse completion test (DCT) and a cued response multiple-choice DCT. The semi-direct measures were to involve a more cued response language laboratory DCT spoken sample and a free response face-to-face structured interview. The self-assessment measures include a cued response rating scale of how the subjects believed they would perform in situations depicted in the DCT and a freer response scale for the subjects to evaluate their performance in a taped interview setting. Thus, the framework did not include formats that were a totally "cued" semi-direct format, such as a multiple-choice language laboratory DCT, because this format did not appear to be a meaningful or productive test type. Likewise, the framework did not include a completely "free" response self-assessment format. Such a format would not provide interpretable data. Consequently, the formats are viewed as being on a scale of more to less free/cued responses. The relationships among the instruments are shown in Figure 1. These different instruments and methods were developed in order to allow examination of variability due to the data collection procedures.

Figure 1: Classification of test methods

	Cued Response	Free Response
Paper and Pencil Indirect Measures	Multiple choice or cued items following situation description DCT	Open ended response following situation description DCT
Oral Semi-direct Measures	Listening laboratory tape response to descriptions of situations	Structured oral interview and response to video-taped scenarios
Self-assessment Measures	Self assessment of performance on situation description	Direct observation and evaluation of the video-taped role play and interview

The process of determining which variables to include in the tests resulted in the selection of power (P), social distance (D), and degree of imposition (R) as the variables of interest. These variables were selected because within the research on cross-cultural pragmatics, they are identified as the three independent and culturally sensitive variables that subsume all other variables and play a principled role in speech act behavior (Brown and Levinson, 1987; also see Fraser, 1990). The definitions and descriptions of the variables used here are as follows:

Relative power (P)

The power of the speaker with respect to the hearer. In effect, this is the degree to which the speaker can impose his or her will on the hearer due to a higher rank within an organization, professional status, or the hearer's need to have a particular duty or job performed.

+P= Speaker has a higher rank, title or social position, or is in control of the assets in the situation. Examples would be a supervisor, manager, president, or customer.

−P= Speaker has a lower/ lesser rank, title or social position, or is not in control of the assets in the situation. Examples would be a worker of lesser status, member of an organization with lesser status, or salesperson serving a customer.

The distance between the speaker and the hearer. In effect, the degree of familiarity and solidarity they share as represented through in-group or out-group membership.

+D= Speaker and hearer do not know or identify with each other. They are strangers interacting due to social/life circumstances. Examples would be customer to service person or law enforcement officer to citizen.

–D= Speaker and hearer know and or identify with each other. There is an affiliation between the speaker and the hearer; they share solidarity in the sense that they could be described as working toward a common goal or interest. Examples would be co-workers or people who belong to the same social or professional organization or club.

Absolute ranking of imposition (R)

The imposition in the culture, in terms of the expenditure of goods and/or services by the hearer, or the obligation of the speaker to perform the act. This will vary depending upon whether the speech act is a request, a refusal, or an apology.

Requests:

+R= Great expenditure of goods, services, or energy required by hearer to carry out the request.

–R= Small expenditure of goods, services, or energy required by hearer to carry out the request.

Refusals:

+R= Great expenditure of goods, services, or energy requested of the speaker.

–R= Small expenditure of goods, services, or energy requested of the speaker.

Apologies:

+R= Great severity of offense or speaker's obligation to apologize is great.

–R= Small severity of offense or speaker's obligation to apologize is small.

Finally, in order to utilize the speech acts most generally researched to date, the speech acts of requests, refusals, and apologies were selected as the speech acts to be investigated. These speech acts are appropriate for contrasting English and Japanese speech act realization, as shown in the literature (see

Hudson, Detmer, and Brown, 1992 for discussion). By incorporating the three pragmatic variables and the particular speech acts just mentioned, it was hoped that the forms of assessment developed could be utilized by many different researchers interested in various areas of cross-cultural pragmatics.

The rationale for developing instruments of different types and methods for application across different social variables and speech acts evolved from an interest in determining the potential differential effectiveness of the instruments. For example, certain speech acts may be effectively assessed better by one method than by another. Apologies may be effectively assessed by self-assessment while requests may not be. Further, apologies that involve such power relationships as a worker apologizing to an employer may be more effectively evaluated by self-assessment than when the power relationships are different. Additionally, the different types of instruments were developed in recognition of the fact that different types of research into cross-cultural pragmatics will require different levels of detail. An examination of the formulaic structure of apologies may be adequately served by an open-ended indirect DCT. On the other hand, research into the effects of interpersonal interaction on apologies may be better served by direct observation in an interview.

Table 1: Variable distribution across tests

Speech Act	Cell Number & Attributes							
Request	1	2	3	4	5	6	7	8
Refusal	9	10	11	12	13	14	15	16
Apology	17	18	19	20	21	22	23	24
Variables								
Imposition	+	+	+	+	−	−	−	−
Power	+	+	−	−	+	+	−	−
Distance	+	−	+	−	+	−	+	−

To sum up, the variables of P, D, and R were to be examined in the speech acts of refusals, requests, and apologies. In order to specify how the variables were to be sampled, specifications delineating how the sociopragmatic variables would be distributed across speech acts were formulated. The purpose of these specifications was to detail which linguistic units serve as the basis of measurement and how they are to be sampled. This framework was designed for use with each method of testing. In examining the interactions of variables and speech acts, 24 cells were identified as being of interest. The cells are indicated in Table 1. The designation of the cells as shown in Table 1 allows an examination of the interaction between sociopragmatic variables and particular speech act realizations. Additionally, this framework permits an examination of each particular variable within each speech act.

The DCT was adopted as the motivator for the development of the other test instruments. As will be seen in the discussion, this was an important decision which we believe has enhanced the quality of the overall project. Given the importance of the DCT in generating the instruments, a detailed discussion of the evaluation process is presented below.

DEVELOPMENT OF DCT INSTRUMENTS

THE DEVELOPMENT OF THE FINAL VERSION of the DCT involved several stages. These stages included the writing, piloting, and revising of item specifications, the writing of DCT items, and the development of three alternate forms of the DCT. The following discussion in this section presents the stages involved in the development and analysis of the open-ended and multiple-choice forms of the DCT.

DEVELOPMENT AND ANALYSIS OF PILOT OPEN-ENDED DCT

After the variable distributions described in Table 1 were determined, initial item specifications were developed (see Appendix A for the final version of the DCT item specifications). These item specifications generally follow the guidelines identified by Popham (1978), and included a general description, sample item, prompt attributes, and response attributes. Following this, test items were generated based upon the specifications. In the initial pilot version, the item writing involved the production of 48 pilot test items for the free response DCT described above. These items were distributed across two 24 item alternate forms of the instrument, designated as Form A and Form B. Table 2 shows the correspondence of the cells to the situations that were generated for each of those cells in the DCT forms. Further, these situation numbers correspond to item numbers across all forms and versions of the paper and pencil instruments. The framework for identifying P, D, and R that was used in generating the test forms is presented in Table 3 and Table 4. This framework corresponds to the final version of the DCT. Each of the two forms was rated by four native speakers of English as to the speech act and whether each item was plus or minus P, D, and R. Additionally, Form A was administered to eight native speakers of English and five non-native speakers

(Japanese). Form B was administered to eight native speakers of English and 12 non-native speakers (Japanese). The results of the analyses on the pilot data are presented below.

Table 2: Cell and situation correspondence across instruments

Requests	cell	1	2	3	4	5	6	7	8
	sit	23	14	3	22	8	16	12	85
Refusals	cell	9	10	11	12	13	14	15	16
	sit	10	9	15	17	21	20	24	4
Apologies	cell	17	18	19	20	21	22	23	24
	sit	6	13	2	7	18	1	11	19

Table 3: Frameworks for power and distance relationships on final version

	+ POWER	– POWER
+ DISTANCE	loan officer customs officer loan officer manager customer customer customer customer	renter traveler loan applicant job applicant salesperson shop worker restaurant staff bank teller
– DISTANCE	supervisor department head project leader lead teacher lease-holder club president	worker department worker project head teacher house-mate club member

Table 4: Framework for degree of imposition of acts in final version

+ IMPOSITION	– IMPOSITION
REQUESTS AND REFUSALS	

do extra work
do work faster
make a decision faster
give more time to finish work
reschedule an important meeting
stay late at work
reschedule with a busy person
stay home all morning waiting for
    a repair person
go on a tour
move furniture in the house
allow a party in your house
	deliver a message
	give change
	talk for a few minutes
	watch a short video
	move out of someone's path
	get/give
	    napkin
	    application form
	    menu
	    item from display case
	    information
	        location of item
	        phone number
	borrow/lend:
	    pen
	    paper
	    paper clip
	    sun screen
	accept:
	    water
	    bubble gum
	    coupon book

APOLOGIES	

destroying property
  papers
  computer files
  vacuum cleaner
  merchandise in a store
  clothing
losing property
  hiking book
  computer disk
failing to follow through with a
  promise to a co-worker:
    at a paid position
    at a volunteer position
	knocking over but not destroying:
	  vase
	  picture
	  ceramic figure
	  menus
	  desk calendar
	  umbrella
	making someone wait a few minutes

Native Speaker Ratings

The native speakers (NS; native speakers=NNS) provided only general agreement with the initial cell designations. Their agreement was 92% with the speech act designation, 81% with power designations, 90% with distance designations and 84% with degree of imposition designations (see Table 5).

Table 5: NS agreement with cell designations

Category of Agreement	Percent Agreement
Speech Act	92%
Power Relationship	81%
Distance Relationship	90%
Degree of Imposition	84%

Examination of the NS rating results produced several implications concerning the *a priori* cell designations and definitions of pragmatic traits. First, the disagreements on the speech act designations tended to occur with situations which later were found to elicit more than one speech act. For example, Item 3 for Form A was designated as a request, but in practice it also elicited an apology in order to carry out the speech act (see Appendix B for a summary of Native Speaker rating problems). Second, there was an apparent interaction between P and D within some of the cells. This was particularly the case when the *a priori* cell designation for an item was minus D. In rating power, the NSs disagreed with the planned P relationship 19% of the time. Of these disagreements, 74% involved cells which had been designated as +P but were rated as –P by the NSs. However, 62% of the total disagreements were in the –D items. This finding regarding –D items is important in that there was agreement on ratings of D 90%. of the time. These results suggest 1) that, while social distance is being rated consistently, power relationships are difficult to determine, and 2) that those power relationships within the minus social distance (–D) situations are very tenuous for English speakers. The NS disagreements with our ratings for degree of imposition tended to occur in cells which we had designated as high imposition (+R) but the raters designated as low imposition situations (–R). These accounted for 77% of the disagreements. This does not appear to be affected by P or D interactions. Of the possible 4 combinations of +/–P by +/–D, 25% of the disagreements occurred in each. Table 6 provides the numbers of coding disagreements with the predicted designations that the native speakers had for the speech acts, P, D, or R referenced to the cell P, D, and R designations. Due to the obvious differences between intended and perceived values of degree of power, distance, and imposition for some of the items, particularly in the +P category, revisions were made. These item revisions are discussed below.

Table 6: Number of NS coding disagreements on Speech Act (SA), Power (P), Distance (D), and Degree of Imposition (R) according cell designations

Cell Designation	Number of NS Disagreements			
P D R	SA	P	D	R
− − −	0	1	3	1
− − +	1	2	2	9
− + −	5	3	3	3
− + +	3	3	4	4
+ − −	1	12	0	1
+ + −	1	5	2	2
+ + +	1	2	4	6

NS and NNS DCT Data Analysis and Results

The data from the DCT were analyzed using a coding scheme based on a combination of the Cross Cultural Speech Act Realization Project (CCSARP) coding system in Blum-Kulka, House, and Kasper (1989) and the system used by Beebe, Takahashi, and Uliss-Weltz (1990) in their study of refusals. For the present study, problematic areas were identified in cases where these coding schemes were inconsistent, unparallel, or did not address speech act realizations in the current data set. Thus, the two coding schemes were revised. Speech act realizations in the current study, including strategy types that were not included in the original categories, were found most often in the non-native speaker data. We can hypothesize that the different strategy types used were due to L1 transfer. In the present study, coding was carried out using the revised scheme indicated in Table 7.

The strategies that emerged, both those common to all speech acts and those specific to particular speech acts, are displayed in Table 7 in the relative order in which they were most often used. Although the original coding scheme included other strategies than those listed, since they did not appear in the present study, they are not reported here. The five alerters were most often used toward the beginning of the speech act realization and were common to all three speech acts. The number of head acts varied according to the speech act elicited: five for requests, nine for refusals, and fourteen for apologies.

Table 7: Reference table of all strategies used by speech act

REQUESTS	REFUSALS	APOLOGIES
Alerters		
	attention getters surname first name undetermined name title/role	
Head Acts	Head Acts	Head Acts

preparatory
strong hint
want statement
hedged performative
statement of fact
	grounder
	statement of regret
	non-performative
	repetition of original
	  request
	request for help
	wish
	set condition for
	  past/future accept
	guilt trip
	repetition of part of
	  request
	hedging
	alternative
	alternative said as a
	  command
		IFID
		(I'm sorry)
		I'm afraid
		I apologize for
		forgive me
		excuse me
		explanation
		offer of repair
		taking responsibility
		statement of fact
		promise forbearance
		minimize offense
		express gratitude
		distract from offense

Supportive Moves	Supportive Moves	

imposition minimizer
grounders
disarmers
preparator
getting pre-commitment
apology
	imposition minimizer
	indirect requests
	statement of empathy
	pause filler
	statement of positive
	  gratitude/appreciate
	emphasis of
	  requester's costs	

Modifications	Modifications	Modifications
Downgraders	*Downgraders*	*Downgraders*
politeness markers	politeness markers	politeness markers
subjectivizer	subjectivizer	subjectivizer
hedge	hedge	hedge
downtoner	appealer	appealer
pause filler		pause filler
		understater
to head act:		cajoler
conditional		
aspect		
tense		
subjunctive		
negation or		
prep.		
Upgraders	*Upgraders*	*Upgraders*
intensifier	intensifier	intensifier
lexical uptoner	emotional expression	emotional expression
emphasis	lexical uptoner	commitment
		indicator

Request and refusal realizations also showed a total of six types of supportive moves each. Modifications, such as *downgraders* and *upgraders*, were used across all three speech acts; however, the types of modifications varied by speech act. For example, a number of the *downgraders* were coded for the requests only because their use carries more significance in that speech act. Likewise, illocutionary force indicating devices (IFIDs) such as "I'm afraid", "I'm sorry", "forgive me", etc. occur only with apologies. Depending on their type, modifications were found throughout the alerters, head acts, and supportive moves. For further explanation and examples of the strategies and a listing of their codes, refer to Appendix C. For more complete discussions, see Blum-Kulka, House, and Kasper (1989) and Beebe, Takahashi, and Uliss-Weltz (1990).

The strategies were tallied and examined for interesting and relevant qualitative trends pertaining to NS/NNS differences in responses. Analysis was carried out for each cell. This analysis determined how the strategy types were being combined in each NS and NNS realization for each of the original 48 situations. The three examples discussed below in Table 8, Table 9, and Table 10 show the application of the coding scheme to actual NS and NNS realizations. The three examples also illustrate the effect of the cell designation on the large variability of NS and NNS performance, from very similar in Example One to divergent in Example Two.

Table 8: NS/NNS item realization Example One:
Request: – Power, – Distance, – Imposition (–P –D –R)

Example One: Test item

> **Situation**: You are a member of a student organization. You are in a meeting now. You would like to take some notes, but you do not have a pen. The president of the organization is sitting next to you and might have an extra pen.
>
> You: _____
>
> _____
>
> President: Sure. Here you go. Keep it, I have another one.

Example One: Coded responses (ordered responses used by 8 NSs and 5 NNSs)

	NATIVE SPEAKERS					
1	att	pr				
2	att	pr/cd				
3		pr/cd				
4		pr				
5		pr/cd				
6		pr				
7	att	pr/cd				
8	att	pr/cd				
	NON-NATIVE SPEAKERS					
1	att	pr				
2	att	pr				
3	att	pr				
4	att	pr/cd				
5		pr/cd				

Example One: Uncoded responses

NATIVE SPEAKERS	
1	Psst. Can I borrow a pen?
2	Excuse me, do you have a pen I could borrow?
3	Could I borrow a pen?
4	Do you have an extra pen?
5	Do you have an extra pen I could use?
6	Do you have an extra pen?
7	Excuse me, do you have a pen I could borrow?
8	Excuse me, do you have a pen I could borrow?
NON-NATIVE SPEAKERS	
1	Excuse me. do you have an extra pen?
2	Excuse me. Do you have an extra pen?
3	Excuse me. Do you have an extra pen for me?
4	Excuse me. but could you lend me a pen?
5	Could I borrow your extra pen?

Example One (Table 8) shows the data and coding of NS and NNS responses to a request item on Form A which was designated as a –P –D –R cell. For this particular cell, the NNSs performance was very similar to that of the NSs. It should be noted that this pattern was also obtained on Form B for the same cell designation.

Table 9: NS/NNS item realization Example Two:
Apology: – Power, + Distance, + Imposition (–P +D +R)

Example Two: Coded responses

> Situation: You are applying for a job in a small company.
> You go into the office to turn in your application form
> to the manager. You talk to the manager for a few minutes,
> but when you move to give the manager your form, you acci-
> dentally knock over an expensive vase on the desk.
>
> You: _____
>
> _____
>
> Manager: Okay, but it's very expensive.

(continued)

Example Two: Coded responses (ordered responses used by 8 NSs and 12 NNSs)

	NATIVE SPEAKERS					
1		sr/i	repair			
2	emo	sr/i				
3	emo	slf. blm	repair			
4	emo	sr	repair			
5	emo	sr/i	repair	sr/i		
6	emo	sr/i	slf. blm	polite	forgive	
7	emo	sr/i	pause	repair	pause	repair
8	emo	sr/i				
	NON-NATIVE SPEAKERS					
1	emo	sr/i	<emphas	up. off/i		
2		dismay	<emphas	sr/i		
3	emo	sr/i	concern	dismay	concern	
4	emo	sr	dismay	sr		
5	emo	slf. blm	<emphas	sr/i	repair	
6		sr/i	slf. blm	repair		
7		sr	dismay	repair		
8	emo	sr/i	dismay	repair		
9	emo	sr	repair			
10		sr	repair			
11	emo	forgive	title	repair		
12		apol	repair			

Example Two: Uncoded responses

	NATIVE SPEAKERS
1	I'm terribly sorry. Can I pay for it?
2	Oh, my God! I'm terribly sorry.
3	Oh my gosh! how clumsy of me. I'll be more than willing to reimburse you for the damage although it may have more than monetary value.
4	Oh, my gosh! I'm sorry. I'll buy you a new one.
5	Oh no! I'm really sorry. Here let me help pick this up. I'm really sorry.

6	Oh, I'm so sorry! How clumsy of me. Please accept my apologies.
7	Oh, I'm so sorry... uh, let me clean it up... uh, I can pay for a new one.
8	Oh, I'm so sorry.

	NON-NATIVE SPEAKERS
1	Oh! I'm VERY SORRY. This must have been very expensive.
2	What have I done! I'm terribly sorry.
3	Oh, I'm very sorry. Didn't you get hurt? What shall I do? Is it expensive?
4	Oh no, I'm sorry. I don't know what to do. I'm sorry.
5	Oh, how stupid I am! I'm terribly sorry. I'll pay for it.
6	I'm so sorry. It's my mistake. Can I pay for the damage?
7	I'm sorry. What should I do? If I can buy some one, I'll buy one.
8	Oh! I'm really sorry. What can I do? I'll pay for it.
9	Oh! I'm sorry. I'll pay.
10	I'm sorry. Can I pay for your vase?
11	Oh no! I beg your pardon, sir. Might I buy the same vase as one.
12	I apologize then let's me pay this.

Example Two (Table 9) shows the results of a –P +D +R apology item. Here the NNS responses were relatively close to the NSs' in many respects. However, 42% of the NNSs (subjects 2, 3, 4, 7, and 8) utilized a statement of or question conveying *dismay* in their realizations. This strategy, however, was never used by the NSs. Its lack of use by NSs and its exclusion from the two original coding schemes suggest that this strategy may be the result of some type of L1 transfer specific to Japanese NNSs.

Table 10: NS/NNS item realization Example Three: Refusal: + Power, – Distance, + Imposition (+P –D +R)

Example Three: Test item

> **Situation:** You are president of a student organization. You have a meeting scheduled with another member for this afternoon. You are sitting outside of the library when the member comes over and asks to cancel the meeting in order to work on a term paper that is due tomorrow. You cannot schedule the meeting for later because you have to report the information to several professors at a meeting tomorrow.

(continued)

You: _____
     _____
     _____

Member: I understand. See you this afternoon then.

Example Three: Coded responses (ordered responses used by 8 NSs and 12 NNSs)

	NATIVE SPEAKERS					
1		gr	imp. min			
2	lex. up	np/i	alt	gr		
3		emp/i	emp	gr	gr/i	rq. hlp
4	und. nam	gr	gr			
5		np/i	gr			
6	hedge	gr	rep. rq			
7	hedge	gr/i				
8		gr/i	imp. min			
	NON-NATIVE SPEAKERS					
1		wish	gr	rg		
2		emp	gr			
3	hedge	emp	np	gr	polite	imp. mn
4		emp	np	gr	imp. min	
5		emp	gr	np		
6		emp	gr	np	rep. rq	
7		rg	np	gr	rep. rq	
8		np	gr			
9		rg	np	gr		
10		rep. rq	gr			
11		rg	np	gr–gr	rep. rq	imp. m
12		rg	gr	np		

Example Three: Uncoded responses

NATIVE SPEAKERS	
1	We have to meet today because I have to report to the board tomorrow. I'll try to make it as short as possible.
2	Look, I really can't reschedule. Couldn't we just try to get things done as quickly as possible this afternoon? I've got to get this information to those professors.
3	I can really sympathize with you I know the feeling well. However, my meeting with the professors requires the information no later than tomorrow at ten a.m. and I need your data to compile my report. It's very important that I have that information. I need your help on this.
4	But, name, we need to meet today. I have to report to a bunch of professors at a meeting tomorrow, so we need to talk today.
5	I really can't reschedule because I need the information for another meeting tomorrow.
6	Unnn, the problem that I have with that is that I have to report this information to several professors tomorrow. Can't we try to squeeze this in?
7	Well, unfortunately, I really need to meet with you today since I have to report to Dr. Prof, Prof, and Prof tomorrow about what we talked about.
8	It's really important that I discuss a few things with you it won't take long.
NON-NATIVE SPEAKERS	
1	I wish I could postpone it for you but I have to report the information to several professors tomorrow at a meeting. I'm sorry about that.
2	I know how things are (at the end of the term) but we have to report what we decide today to some professors tomorrow.
3	Well, I understand your situation but we cannot delay the schedule because I must make a report by tomorrow. Please, it won't take long.
4	I understand that you are busy, but I can't reschedule the meeting because I have to report the information to professors at a meeting tomorrow. The meeting shouldn't be long, so...
5	I know you want to study, but I have to report to professors about the meeting so I can't cancel it.

6	I understand, but I already informed to professors at our meeting today. I think it cannot be canceled. Would you attend the meeting this afternoon?
7	Sorry. I can't change. Because I have to report for tomorrow meeting. Can you have meeting this afternoon?
8	We cannot cancel the meeting so we have to report the information to several professors.
9	I'm sorry but we can't change day because I have to turn in report to professors tomorrow.
10	Is it possible to keep a meeting? I have to report to several professors tomorrow.
11	I'm sorry I can't change our meeting because I have to report the information to several professors at a meeting tomorrow. It's my important work. Can you come to the room a short time?
12	I'm sorry. I've already scheduled so I can't change the day.

The data from Example Three are presented in Table 10 and represent responses to a refusal item which was coded as +P −D +R. Here the NS and NNS realizations show a number of differences. At times, the NNS realizations lack the same strategy types used by the NSs. For example, the NSs were using some type of alerter 50% (subjects 2, 4, 6, and 7) of the time, while NNS use fell to 8% (subject 3). Likewise, 63% of the NS responses (those of subjects 2, 3, 5, 7, and 8) were upgraded with an *intensifier* (in one case, two), yet not one NNS response included an *intensifier*. Other differences between NS and NNS responses for this situation show NNSs use of strategies not employed by the NSs (as in Example Two). NNSs were using either the *empathy* or the *regret* strategies in 84% of their responses (subjects 1–7, 9, 11, and 12), while NSs were using the *empathy* and the *regret* strategies in 13% (subject 3) and 0% of their responses respectively. Finally, the repetition of the original request strategy was employed in 33% of the NNS responses (subjects 6, 7, and 11) compared to 13% (subject 6) in the NS responses.

Thus, as expected, the degree of similarity between NS and NNS performance for speech act realization depended upon the situation and how the variables of P, D, and R interacted with the particular speech act.

Changes to Specific Items Based on the NS and NNS DCT Results

Throughout the process of analyzing the DCT data, it became clear that, although most items were productive, some items were not performing as intended. The problem items generally fell into one of three areas. The first area was the elicitation of the wrong speech act. For example, for one apology item, the situation itself required so much processing that many of the subject responses did not include an apology. Apparently, the subjects were reacting to parts of the described situation other than the apology elicitation. Another apology item was performing too much like a request item. The second problem area appeared when subjects opted out of responding to the speech act. Opting out generally occurred with refusal items which involved such a low degree of imposition that the respondents were in a position where they did not see a need to refuse the request. The last problematic area resulted from respondents' misinterpretations of the P, D, and R relationships in certain items. For example, in some situations requiring the examinee to interact with office personnel, it was not clear to the respondents that the office staff was in a position of power. The problematic items were rewritten in order to repair the difficulties that were identified. See Appendix D for specific examples of problematic items.

Changes in Item Specifications Based on NS and NNS DCT Results

In addition to changes to specific items, several modifications were made to the item specifications based on the analysis of the NS and NNS data. For example, on the pilot versions of the instruments, the answers that were to be supplied by the examinees were followed by a written response prompt such as "Thank you", as is common in the DCT format. These prompts were dropped from the revised items because they appeared to frequently interfere with realistic and appropriate test-taker generated responses.

In addition to deleting the final response prompt, several constraints on prompt construction were also added to the item specifications. One such constraint involved making sure of examinee familiarity with situations. For example, it was found that several of the Japanese subjects were unfamiliar with the situation of student organizations. This required changes in the specification for the types of organizations to be included in the test forms. Another constraint on item specifications that emerged was the need to avoid professionally defined or formulaic interactions. For example, doctor and patient interaction or an interaction between a customer and a movie ticket seller require a very restricted interaction, and thus are not appropriate for the present type of measures. Finally, it was decided that all situations should be explicitly context-internal. For example, if the roles of the interlocutors are project leader to project worker, the context of the speech event must be at work rather than at a social event. This constraint was designed to ensure that the posited social distance relationships remained constant.

DEVELOPMENT AND ANALYSIS OF REVISED PILOT INSTRUMENTS

As described above, the initial ratings of plus and minus P, D, and R values, along with the results of the data analysis of NS and NNS responses to the DCT Version #1, led to revisions of specific items and overall item specifications. These revisions were incorporated in the three forms (A, B, and C) of the second version of the DCT. DCT Version #2 was administered to a slightly larger sample of subjects than the first version. A total of twenty-eight NSs of English were tested; nine each on Forms A and B, and ten on Form C. A total of twelve NNSs (Japanese) were tested; four on each form. The NS and NNS DCT Version #2 data were analyzed using the Childes/Clan language analysis program, the *SPSS* statistical analysis program (Norusis 1988), and the *Quatro Pro* spreadsheet program (Borland International, Inc. 1987). The analysis was carried out to determine whether there were systematic differences in the responses of NSs and NNSs, and whether these differences could be incorporated into the multiple-choice DCT and other scales. Results of this analysis are discussed below.

NS and NNS Strategy Use Overall and by Cell

The results of the strategies used overall and for particular cells follow and are broken down into two sections: strategies specific to particular speech acts and strategies common across speech acts. Low use cases — those for which a strategy showed less than 10% use for NS (fewer than 3 uses) and less than 16.9% use for NNSs (fewer than 2 uses) on a given cell — were excluded from the analysis. In the tables shown below, however, if a strategy had high use by one group (either NSs or NNSs), then the use by the other group is displayed even if its use was low. Also, in the tables, there are two averages displayed: one average excludes low use strategies (labeled "High Use Average"), and the other average includes the low use strategies (labeled "NS/NNS Breakdown" of total average).

Strategies Specific to Particular Speech Acts

In general, if a strategy was used by the NSs, it was also used by the NNSs (excluding the low use cases). However, of the three speech acts, the strategies used in the apology situations showed more variation in use. Also, for all three speech acts, many more strategies were used in the +R cells than the –R cells. Consequently, greater variance was generally observed between NS and NNS strategy use for the +R cells compared to –R cells. The following discussion presents the strategies for each of the speech acts of requests, refusals, and apologies.

Table 11: NS and NNS strategy use overall and high use by cell for requests

| Strategies | Overall Use | | | Use by Cell with R, P, and D Designations | | | | | | | | High Use |
Head Acts	Total Average	NS/NNS Breakdown		1 +++	2 ++-	3 +-+	4 +--	5 -++	6 -+-	7 --+	8 ---	Average
Prepar-atory	82.6	NS	77.7	64.3	46.4	75.0	82.1	100.0	100.0	53.6	96.4	77.7
		NNS	87.5	66.7	66.7	83.3	100.0	100.0	100.0	75.0	100.0	87.5
Want/Like	7.6	NS	8.9	3.6	28.6	17.9				17.9		8.5
		NNS	6.3	25.0	0.0	16.7				8.3		6.3
State Facts	6.8	NS	8.5	46.4	14.3							7.6
		NNS	5.2	16.7	16.7							4.2
Strong Hint	4.2	NS	5.4			3.6	10.7			17.9		4.0
		NNS	3.1			16.7	0.0			0.0		2.1

(continued)

Table 11 (cont.): NS and NNS strategy use overall and high use by cell for requests

Supportive Moves	Total Average	NS/NNS Breakdown	1 +++	2 ++-	3 +-+	4 +--	5 -++	6 -+-	7 --+	8 ---	High Use Average
Ground	55.5	NS	45.1	39.3	67.9	75.0	96.4	0.0	21.4	17.9	42.9	45.1
		NNS	65.8	75.0	91.7	91.7	100.0	18.2	33.3	41.7	66.7	65.8
Apology	10.5	NS	11.6	39.3		10.7	35.7					10.7
		NNS	9.4	41.7		8.3	16.7					8.3
Disarm	8.9	NS	6.3		21.4	25.0	0.0					5.8
		NNS	11.5		25.0	41.7	16.7					10.4
Prep	8.5	NS	7.6		39.3		7.1					5.8
		NNS	9.4		41.7		33.3					9.4
Impos Mini	3.1	NS	3.1	7.1	10.7							2.2
		NNS	3.1	16.7	0.0							2.1

NNSs relied more heavily on the *preparatory* head act than did the NSs, and thus narrowed their repertoire of head act strategies, as shown in Table 11. The supportive move of *grounder* was in high use across almost all cells for both the NSs and the NNSs. In general, the NNSs used more supportive moves than the NSs did. *Apologies, disarmers,* and *preparators* had consistent use on specific cells. NS and NNS responses to the –R cells often consisted of only two strategies, most often a *preparatory* and *grounder*, whereas the +R cells added a variety of head act and supportive move strategies.

Head Acts

The *preparatory* strategy was very heavily used by NSs and NNSs on all cells, with averages of 77.7% and 87.5%, respectively. However, as mentioned above, NNS use was consistently higher than NS use (particularly on cells 2, 4, and 7). The *want/like* strategy use varied for each cell. NNS use dominated on cell 1 (NNSs 25.0%, NSs 3.6%). However, there was high NS use on cell 2 (NSs 28.6%, NNSs 0%) and cell 7 (NSs 17.9%, NNSs 8.3%). NSs and NNSs performed similarly on cell 3, at 17.9%, and 16.7%, respectively. Use of *statement of facts* fell into cells 1 and 2, with higher NS use on cell 1 (46.4% to 16.7%) and similar use on cell 2 (14.3% and 16.7%). *Strong hints* were used mainly on cells 3, 4, and 7, with NNS use only on cell 3 (NNSs 16.7%, NSs 3.6%). NS use on cells 4 and 7 was at 10.7% and 17.9%, respectively.

Supportive Moves

Grounders had regular use by NSs and NNSs across almost all cells, with the exception of cell 5 for NSs. NNS use exceeded NS use on all cells, with averages of 65.8% and 45.1%, respectively. *Apologies* were used similarly by NSs and NNSs on cell 1 (NSs 39.3%, NNSs at 41.7%) and cell 3 (NSs 10.7%, NNSs at 8.3%). However, NS use exceed NNS use on cell 4, with averages of 35.7% for NSs compared to 16.7% for NNSs. *Disarmers* were used on cells 2, 3, and 4, with NNS use always greater than NS use — cell 2, 25.0% and 21.4%; cell 3, 41.7% and 25.0%; cell 4, 16.7% and 0%, respectively. *Preparators* were used on cell 2, with fairly equal use between NSs and NNSs, at 39.3% and 41.7%, respectively; and cell 4, with NNSs use at 33.3% compared to a low 7.1% by the NSs. *Imposition Minimizers* had 16.7% use by NNSs and 7.1% use by NSs on cell 1, and 10.7% use by NSs on cell 2 (no NNS use of *minimizers* for cell 2).

Considering use of both head act and supportive moves, NS and NNS use differed most significantly on cell 4, a –P –D +R cell. Apparently the specific variable values of the cell had a role to play in explaining the difference in NS and NNS realization. Here the NNSs opted for the *preparatory* alone while the NS used both the *preparatory* and the *strong hint*. NNSs used a greater variety of supportive moves than NSs, primarily *grounders*, *disarmers*, and *preparators*. NSs relied on the *grounder* and the *apology*, however. NS and NNS performance also differed on cell 2, a +P –D +R cell.

Thus, it seems that the NNSs were fairly competent in their performance on –R cells. Nonetheless, they did show an over-dependence on the *preparatory* strategy. Since this strategy was found to be common to NSs as well, the preparatory seems to be a "safe" strategy for NNSs in doubt. Perhaps due to their consistent over-reliance on the *preparatory* head act strategy, NNSs compensated through more use and variation of the supportive move strategies. Or perhaps NNSs felt more need to support their requests than NSs did. To conclude, systematic differences were found between NS and NNS performance on the speech act of Request.

Refusals

With refusals, NSs and NNSs basically used the same strategies on the same cells. However, some strategies showed higher NNS use, while others showed higher NS use (see Table 12). For overall average use, NNS use exceeded NS use on the head acts of *grounders* (NNSs 92.7%, NSs 86.6%), *regret* (NNSs 60.4%, NSs 46.9%), *non-performatives* (NNSs 40.6%, NSs 30.8%), *wish* (NNSs 11.5%, NSs 5.4%), and *guilt trip* (NNSs 5.2%, NSs 1.8%); and the supportive move of *gratitude* (NNSs 18.8%, NSs 15.6%).

Apparently, *grounders*, when used in refusals, serve as head acts, whereas in requests they function as supportive moves. In a request, if *grounders* are used without a head act, they are then coded as *indirect requests*. For refusals, people often offer reasons for refusing as the sole or key part of the refusal itself.

NS use was slightly greater on the head acts of *alternative* (NSs 35.3%, NNSs 31.3%), *alternative said as a command* (NSs 2.7%, NNSs 2.1%), *set condition for acceptance* (NSs 2.2%, NNSs 2.1%), *repetition of original request* (NSs 2.2%, NNSs 1%), and the supportive move of *imposition minimizer* (NSs 1.3%, NNSs 1%). Concerning specific cell use, when NS and NNS use was equal or very similar, it tended to be on the –R cells. Strategies used in these cells had fairly high use, at 50.0% to 33.3%.

Head Acts and Supportive Moves

The head acts of *grounders*, *regret*, *non-performatives*, and *alternatives* were consistently used by NSs and NNSs across almost all cells (use on cells averaging from 30.8% to 92.7%). *Non-performatives* showed great difference in NS and NNS use on three cells. On cells 9 and 12, NNS use dominated at

Table 12: NS and NNS strategy use overall and high use by cell for refusals

Strategies Head Acts	Total Average	NS/NNS Breakdown	Use by Cell with R, P, and D Designations								High Use Average
			9 +++	10 ++-	11 +-+	12 +--	13 -++	14 -+-	15 --+	16 ---	
Ground	89.7	NS	100.0	85.7	71.4	96.4	75.0	96.4	75.0	89.3	86.6
		NNS	83.3	91.7	100.0	100.0	83.3	91.7	83.3	100.0	92.7
Regret	53.6	NS	46.4	35.7	60.7	53.6	39.3	21.4	67.9	50.0	46.9
		NNS	33.3	50.0	83.3	83.3	58.3	50.0	75.0	50.0	60.4
NonPer	35.7	NS	39.3	35.7	32.1	28.6	39.3	25.0	25.0	21.4	30.8
		NNS	75.0	41.7	25.0	66.7	41.7	33.3	33.3	8.3	40.6
Altern	33.3	NS	17.9	42.9	67.9	57.1		39.3	35.7	21.4	35.3
		NNS	25.0	25.0	25.0	66.7		33.3	16.7	50.0	30.2
Wish	8.4	NS	10.7	7.1	3.6	21.4					5.4
		NNS		25.0	16.7	33.3					9.4
Guilt	3.5	NS	14.3								1.8
		NNS	41.7								5.2
Alt/ Command	2.4	NS		21.4							2.7
		NNS		16.7							2.1
Set Cond	2.2	NS		14.3							1.8
		NNS		8.3							1.0
Rep. of Request	1.6	NS	17.9								2.2
		NNS	8.3								1.0

(continued)

Table 12 (cont.): NS and NNS strategy use overall and high use by cell for refusals

Supportive Moves	Total Average	NS/NNS Breakdown		9 +++	10 ++-	11 +-+	12 +--	13 -++	14 -+-	15 --+	16 ---	High Use Average
Gratitude	17.2	NS	15.6					32.1	35.7	28.6	28.6	15.6
		NNS	18.8					41.7	33.3	41.7	33.3	18.8
Impos	1.2	NS	1.3		10.7							1.3
Mini		NNS	1.0		8.3							1.0

75.0% and 66.7% compared to NS use at 39.3% and 28.6%, respectively. Additionally, NS use of *non-performatives* surpassed NNS use on cell 16 (NS 21.4%, NNS 8.3%). The supportive move of *gratitude* was common to –R cells only (cells 13 through 16), and when used in a cell, averaged from 28.6% to 41.7% use. NNS use of *gratitude* exceeded NS use in cells 13 and 15, with use at 41.7% compared the NS use of 32.1% and 28.6%, respectively. *Wish* was common to +R cells, being used up to 33.3% for those cells, and showing NNS use of 25.0% compared to NS use of 7.1% on cell 10. Specific to cell 9 were *guilt trip* (NSs 14.3%, NNSs 41.7%) and *repetition of original request* (NSs 8.3%, NNSs 17.9%). Specific to cell 10 were the head acts *alternative as a command* (NSs 21.4%, NNSs 16.7%) and *set condition* (NSs 14.3%, NNSs 8.3%), and the supportive move of *imposition minimizer* (NSs 10.7%, NNSs 8.3%). Thus, the +P/+R cells (9 and 10) had the greatest variety of strategy use. Compared to the other cells, NS and NNS use differed most greatly on cell 9, a +P +D +R cell.

In sum, it seems that, depending on the situation, the NNSs took different approaches than the NSs when handling the face-threatening situations of refusal. In some situations, the NNSs were more likely than the NSs to use more potentially confrontational strategies, such as the *guilt trip* and non-performative strategies in cell 9. In other situations, NNSs seemed to avoid conflict in ways that the NSs did not, as evidenced through higher NS use of the *alternative said as a command* and *set condition* strategies in cell 10. The difference in performance seems to be the result of the position of power; in cell 9, the speakers had a higher position of power, whereas in cell 10, they held less power.

Apologies

For the speech act of apology, the differences between amounts and types of strategies used were not as clear. Some strategies, such as *sorry, grounder,* and *concern for hearer,* were used across all cells, while some were used for the most part only on the +R cells. For example, +R strategies were *offer of repair, admission of facts, afraid, upgrading the offense, not responsible, self blame, gratitude,* and *apologize,* as shown in Table 13. Other strategies were used mainly on the –R cells (cells 21 through 24); these strategies were *lack of intent* and *minimization of offense.* Patterns differentiated by NS and NNS status were rare.

Head Acts

The use of *sorry* was a high use strategy across all cells, with overall averages of 81.3% for NNSs and 73.7% for NSs. NNS use was higher than NS use on all cells except 22 and 23. Both NNS and NS use of

Table 13: NS and NNS strategy use overall and high use by cell for apologies

Strategies Head Acts	Overall Use Total Average	Overall Use NS/NNS Breakdown	Overall Use NS/NNS Breakdown	Use by Cell with R, P, and D Designations 17 +++	18 ++-	19 +-+	20 +--	21 -++	22 -+-	23 --+	24 ---	High Use Average
Sorry	77.5	NS	73.7	92.9	71.4	96.4	25.0	67.9	85.7	67.9	82.1	73.7
		NNS	81.3	100.0	91.7	100.0	41.7	75.0	66.7	66.7	91.7	81.3
Offer Repair	20.3	NS	21.9	39.3	28.6	60.7	28.6	10.7				21.0
		NNS	18.8	33.3	8.3	66.7	41.7	0.0				18.8
Ground	17.6	NS	20.5	10.7	57.1	17.9	17.9		14.3	25.0	17.9	20.1
		NNS	14.6	8.3	50.0	8.3	8.3		16.7	8.3	16.7	14.6
Concer	17.8	NS	14.7	17.9	28.6	32.1	21.4	7.1	3.6		7.1	14.7
		NNS	20.8	33.3	33.3	8.3	0.0	33.3	33.3		16.7	19.8
Admis Facts	11.5	NS	12.5		35.7		50.0					10.7
		NNS	10.4		41.7		25.0					8.3
Distra Task	10.3	NS	11.2			10.7		28.6		39.3		9.8
		NNS	9.4			0.0		33.3		33.3		8.3
Lack of Intent	5.9	NS	7.6					21.4	10.7	14.3	14.3	7.6
		NNS	4.2					16.7	0.0	8.3	0.0	3.1
Afraid	5.3	NS	5.4		17.9	10.7	10.7					4.9
		NNS	5.2		8.3	0.0	25.0					4.2
Up Offens	4.7	NS	6.3		17.9	3.6	21.4					5.4
		NNS	3.1		0.0	16.7	0.0					2.1

Mini Offens	3.2	NS	5.4			14.3	28.6		5.4
		NNS	1.0			0.0	8.3		1.0
Not Respon	3.0	NS	1.8		10.7				1.3
		NNS	4.2		16.7				2.1
Self Blame	2.9	NS	2.7	10.7					1.3
		NNS	3.1	0.0					0.0
Gratitude	2.8	NS	1.3	7.1				3.6	1.3
		NNS	4.2	8.3				25.0	4.2
Apology	1.5	NS	0.9	0.0					0.0
		NNS	2.1	16.7					2.1

sorry was lower on cell 20, a −P −D +R cell (NNSs 41.7%, NSs 25.0%), than on other cells. As noted in the discussion of Table 2 above, cells correspond to situations and items on the three forms of the final version of the open-ended DCT. These forms are presented in Appendix E. *Offer of repair* was used predominately on the +R cells, with its greatest use on cell 19 (−P +D +R), where NS use was 60.7% and NNS use was 66.7%. The NS–NNS dominance of this strategy was split with NS use dominating on +P cells 17, 18, and 21, and NNS use dominating on −P cells 19 and 20. *Grounders* were used across all cells except cell 21 (+P −D −R) and were used more often by the NSs overall (20.5% NS and 14.6% NNS). NS use was especially higher than NNS use on cell 23 (NS 25.0%, NNS 8.3%). *Concern for hearer* was used across all cells except cell 22 and 23 (−P +D −R). NNS use was fairly consistent across the +P cells and averaged 20.8%, whereas NS use was consistent on the +R cells and averaged 14.7%. *Admission of facts* was used only on the +R/−D cells 18 and 20. NNS use was greater for cell 18 (NNSs 41.7%, NSs 35.7%), a −P −D +R cell. NS use was greater for cell 20 (NSs 50.0%, NNSs 25.0%). Predominant use of the *distract with a task-oriented remark* strategy was found on the −R cells 21 and 23. NNS use was greater for cell 21 (NNSs 33.3%, NSs 28.6%). NS use was greater for cell 23 and 19 (NSs 39.3% and 10.7%, and NNSs 33.3% and 0% respectively).

Although several other strategies were used below 10% of the time, they provide some interesting information about NS and NNS strategy use. *Lack of intent* proved to be a −R strategy and had greater use by the NSs than by the NNSs (NSs 7.6%, NNSs 4.2%). *Afraid* was used by NS and NNS on cells 18 through 20, with higher NNS use on cell 20 (NNS 25.0%, NS 10.7), and similar overall averages of 5.4% for NSs and 5.2% for NNSs. *Upgrading offense* was a +R strategy with greater use by NSs on cells 18 and 20, −D cells, (NSs 17.9% and 21.4%, NNSs 0% on both cells). NNSs had greater use on cell 19, a +D cell (NNSs 16.7%, NSs 3.6%). *Minimization of offense* was understandably a −R strategy and was found in cells 21 and 22. NS use dominated both cells (NSs 14.3% and 28.6%, NNSs 0% and 8.3%, respectively). *Not responsible* was used only on cell 20 and was used more by NNSs (16.7%) than NSs (10.7%). *Gratitude* was found in cells 18 and 23 only with greater NNS use on cell 23 (NNSs 25.0%, NSs 3.6%) and similar use on cell 18 (NNSs 8.3%, NSs 7.1%). Generally, then, NSs relied more heavily than NNSs on *concern for hearer*, *admission of facts*, and *upgrading offense*, while NNSs relied on offer of *repair*, *afraid*, and the more conventional *sorry*.

To conclude, differences between NS and NNS use on the −R apology speech act cells showed greater variation than NS and NNS comparisons for the −R request and refusal cells. Although some strategies were found across most cells, many strategies showed very specialized use by NSs and NNSs on specific cells. A few interesting trends were found. For example, NNSs showed focused use of *concern for hearer* on the +P cells, which seemed to indicate a one-way relationship from higher to lower status for this strategy. However, it was generally difficult to find trends in the use of apology strategies.

Summary of Strategies Specific to Particular Speech Acts

Throughout the data for the three speech acts of requests, refusals, and apologies, both similarities and differences in NS and NNS response realization were found. For each speech act, there were a number of strategies that showed high use across all cells regardless of whether the examinee was a NS or a NNS. Such strategies were *preparatory* for requests, *grounder* for refusals, and *sorry* for apologies. Further, for the most part, NS and NNS performance on the –R request and refusal cells was similar. With the introduction of more strategies on the +R cells, however, numerous NS and NNS differences in speech act realizations resulted. The instances of NNS use of specific strategies not found in NS responses were apparently the result of NNS transfer. Examples of this type of transfer were the NNS use of *guilt trip* on refusal cell 9 and the use of *express gratitude* on apology cell 23. Thus, as noted throughout the discussion of the results, trends exist regarding NS and NNS use of strategies depending on the position of power, the degree of distance, and the level of imposition involved in the specific cells.

Strategies Common to All Three Speech Acts

The strategies discussed above were specific to either requests, refusals, or apologies. However, three categories of strategies — alerters, downgraders, and upgraders — were common to all three speech acts. This section discusses the use of such strategies within and across the three speech acts.

The overall use of alerters, downgraders, and upgraders generally showed NSs and NNSs following similar trends on higher use strategies such as the alerter of *attention getters*, the downgraders of *politeness markers* and *conditional*, and the upgraders of *intensifier* and *emotion*. However, in a comparison of NS and NNS overall use on lesser used strategies and use by cell, differences became clear. In addition, some interesting trends were found in NS and NNS use according to the plus and minus P, D, R and distinctions.

Alerters. In the category of alerters, *attention getters* proved to be the strategy with the highest use, with overall averages of 19.8% for NSs and 20.1% for NNSs (see Table 14). The four other alerter strategies that were used had low NS and NNS overall averages from between 1.0% by the NSs for *surname* to 5.2% by the NNSs for *title/role*. NNS use of

Table 14: Averages of alerter use overall and by speech act

Alerter Strategy	Total Average	NS/NNS Breakdown		Speech Act		
				Request	Refusal	Apology
Attention Getter	20.0	NS	19.8	41.1	2.7	15.6
		NNS	20.1	40.6	1.0	18.8
Surname	1.7	NS	1.0	1.3	0.4	1.3
		NNS	2.4	1.0	2.1	4.2
First Name	3.5	NS	3.9	4.5	4.0	3.1
		NNS	3.1	6.3	2.1	1.0
Undetermined Name	3.4	NS	4.8	7.6	1.8	4.9
		NNS	2.1	5.2	1.0	0.0
Title/Role	3.2	NS	1.2	1.8	0.9	0.9
		NNS	5.2	8.3	5.2	2.1

title/role, although low at 5.2%, was much higher than NS use at 1.2% overall. This difference is even greater when comparing NS to NNS use of the strategy on requests (NNS 8.3%, NS 1.8%). However, the use in specific speech acts varied depending upon cell designation. *Attention getters* were used a great deal in requests (averages of NSs at 41.1% and NNSs at 40.6%) and apologies (NS average of 15.6%, and NNS average of 18.8%) (see Table 15). Use of *attention getters* in requests was consistently high across all cells for both NSs and NNSs, with the exception of cells 1 and 7, which had zero NNS use. Thus, NS use dominated on cells 1 (21.4%) and 7 (a high 67.9%). NNS use was greater on cells 2–5, however, with NNS averages spanning 83.3% to 33.3%, and NS averages from 50.0% to 28.6%. NS and NNS performed similarly on cells 6 (NSs 42.9%, NNSs 41.7%) and 8 (NSs 39.3%, NNSs 41.7%). *Attention getters* were used on specific cells for the apologies with slightly greater use on the +R cells overall and varied NS and NNS dominance. NS use exceeded NNS use on cells 18 (NSs 32.1%, NNSs 25.0%) and 22 (NSs 25.0%, NNSs 16.7%), both +P/–D cells, while NNS use greatly exceeded NS use on cells 20 (NNSs 58.3%, NSs 28.6%) and 24 (NNSs 25.0%, NSs 17.9%), both –P/–D cells. NS and NNS use was similar on cells 19 (NS 14.3%, NNS 16.7%) and 23 (NSs 7.1%, NNSs 8.3%).

Minimal or Sporadic Use Alerters. In addition to *attention getting*, other strategies were used though with lower frequency. Generally, NSs

Table 15: Use of *alerters* by cell for requests, refusals and apologies

Strategies		Use by Cell with R, P, and D Designations								High Use
Request Alerters		1	2	3	4	5	6	7	8	Average
		+++	++-	+-+	+--	-++	-+-	--+	---	---
Atten Get	NS	21.4	50.0	28.6	28.6	50.0	42.9	67.9	39.3	41.1
	NNS	0.0	83.3	33.3	66.7	58.3	41.7	0.0	41.7	40.6
First Name	NS		14.3		10.7					3.1
	NNS		16.7		16.7					4.2
Undetermined	NS		17.9		17.9		17.9			6.7
Name	NNS		16.7		8.3		16.7			5.2
Title/Role	NS							10.7		1.3
	NNS							41.7		5.2

Strategies										High Use
Refusal Alerters		9	10	11	12	13	14	15	16	Average
		+++	++-	+-+	+--	-++	-+-	--+	---	---
Title/Role	NS			3.6				0.0		0.4
	NNS			16.7				25.0		5.2
Surname	NS			0.0						0.0
	NNS			16.7						2.1

(continued)

Table 15 (cont.): Use of *alerters* by cell for requests, refusals and apologies

Apology Alerters		17 +++	18 ++-	19 +-+	20 +--	21 -++	22 -+-	23 --+	24 ---	High Use Average
Atten Get	NS		32.1	14.3	28.6		25.0	7.1	17.9	15.6
	NNS		25.0	16.7	58.3		16.7	8.3	25.0	18.8
First Name	NS		10.7		10.7					2.7
	NNS		8.3		0.0					1.0
Undeter-mined Name	NS		17.9		10.7				10.7	4.9
	NNS		0.0		0.0				0.0	0.0
Surname	NS				3.6					0.4
	NNS				16.7					2.1

dominated the use of the less formal *first name* and *undetermined name* strategies, while the NNSs dominated the strategies of *surname* and *title/role*. *First name* and *undetermined name* showed no use at all by NSs or NNSs for the refusal cells. With apologies, NS use exceeded NNS use overall (*first name*, NSs 3.1%, NNSs 1%; *undetermined name*, NSs 4.9%, NNSs 0%), while there was generally more equal use for requests (*first name*, NSs 4.5%, NNSs 6.3%; *undetermined name*, NSs 7.6%, NNSs 5.2%). Cells for which *first name* was used tended to be +R–D cells, while *undetermined name* was used in –D cells. NNSs dominated the use of *surname* and *title/role*. While there was no use of *surname* across the request cells, use of *surname* for refusals was limited to cell 11 (NNSs 16.7%, NSs 0%), and for apologies to cell 20 (NNSs 16.7%, NSs 3.6%). The *title/role* strategy was used on request cell 7, with high NNS use at 41.7% compared to NS use at 10.7%, and refusal –P +D cells 11 (NNSs 16.7%, NSs 3.6%) and 15 (NNSs 25.0%, NSs 0%).

NS and NNS differences in the types of alerter used showed a pattern of greater formality on the part of the NNSs. Native English speaking subjects, perhaps following cultural norms, tended to be less formal, as seen in their use of first names. Japanese native speaking subjects, however, tended to be more formal, as seen in their use of *title/role*. Thus, cultural differences in the degree of formality were found in the NS and NNS realizations of alerters.

To conclude, patterns of *attention getter* use were hard to distinguish. It seems that in some cells, *attention getter* use decreased when the use of other alerters increased. For example, NNS use of *attention getters* dropped to 0% on cell 7, whereas the use of *title/role* jumped to 41.7%. Overall, however, alerters generally showed a trend of higher use on the –D cells for requests and apologies.

Downgraders. Two downgraders, *politeness markers* and *conditional*, were in high use across all request cells with averages for *politeness markers* of 22.3% for NSs, and 19.8% for NNSs, and for *conditional*, NSs at 41.5% and NNSs at 40.6% (see Table 16).

For *politeness markers*, NS use was much greater than NNS use on cells 1 (NSs 32.1%, NNSs 8.3%) and 5 (NSs 39.3%, NNSs 8.3%), both +P/+D cells (see Table 17). NNS use exceeded NS use only on cell 4 (NNSs 33.3%, NSs 7.1%). NSs and NNSs performed very similarly on the other cells. *Politeness markers* were also used in the refusal cell 9 (NSs 7.1%, NNSs at 16.7%). Thus, it appears that although they were generally concerned with politeness, the NNSs were much less concerned with adding politeness strategies when they were in a position of power conversing with people they did not know. *Conditional* was coded only for request cells. NS dominance on most cells (except 2 and 7) was not adequately reflected in the overall averages of 41.5% for NS and 40.6% for NNS.

Minimal or Sporadic Use Downgraders. In general, the downgrader strategies were used only sporadically. *Downtoners* were found in various request and apology cells, usually with NS dominance. Overall averages for requests were 8.5% for NSs and 6.3% for NNSs. Overall averages for

Table 16: Averages of downgrader use overall and by speech act

Downgrader Strategy	Total Average	NS/NNS Breakdown		Speech Act		
				Request	Refusal	Apology
Polite Mark	8.2	NS	9.1	22.3	2.2	2.7
		NNS	7.3	19.8	2.1	0.0
Downtoner	3.6	NS	4.0	8.5	0.4	3.1
		NNS	3.1	6.3	1.0	2.1
Pause Fill	2.9	NS	1.6	0.9	1.3	2.7
		NNS	4.2	9.4	1.0	2.1
Subjunctive	2.7	NS	2.2	1.8	3.6	1.3
		NNS	3.1	2.1	6.3	1.0
Hedge	2.0	NS	1.9	1.8	3.6	0.4
		NNS	2.1	3.1	3.1	0.0
Understater	1.7	NS	1.9	4.0	0.9	0.9
		NNS	1.4	2.1	2.1	0.0
Appealer	1.5	NS	1.3	0.4	2.2	1.3
		NNS	1.7	2.1	3.1	0.0
Request Only Downgraders			Total	Request		
Conditional		NS	13.8	41.5		
		NNS	13.5	40.6		
Aspect		NS	1.5	4.5		
		NNS	3.5	10.4		
Tense		NS	1.5	4.5		
		NNS	2.4	7.3		
Conditional Clause		NS	1.0	3.1		
		NNS	1.4	4.2		

Table 17: Use of *downgraders* by cell for requests, refusals and apologies

Strategies		Use by Cell with R, P, and D Designations								High Use
Request		1	2	3	4	5	6	7	8	Average
Downgraders		+++	++-	+-+	+--	-++	-+-	--+	---	
Polite	NS	32.1	14.3	25.0	7.1	39.3	17.9	14.3	28.6	22.3
	NNS	8.3	16.7	25.0	33.3	8.3	16.7	16.7	33.3	19.8
Downtoner	NS	17.9		14.3				10.7	14.3	7.1
	NNS	8.3		0.0				0.0	25.0	4.2
Pause	NS	0.0		3.6	3.6					0.9
Filler	NNS	16.7		16.7	25.0					7.3
Subjunctive	NS	10.7								1.3
	NNS	16.7								2.1
Understate	NS								21.4	2.7
	NNS								0.0	0.0

(continued)

Table 17 (cont.): Use of *downgraders* by cell for requests, refusals and apologies

Request Only Downgraders		1 +++	2 ++-	3 +-+	4 +--	5 -++	6 -+-	7 --+	8 ---	High Use Average
Conditional	NS	32.1	32.1	64.3	53.6	39.3	35.7	21.4	53.6	41.5
	NNS	25.0	66.7	50.0	41.7	33.3	25.0	41.7	41.7	40.6
Aspect	NS		10.7	14.3	7.1					4.0
	NNS		33.3	16.7	25.0					9.4
Tense	NS		10.7	14.3	7.1					4.0
	NNS		25.0	8.3	16.7					6.3
CondClause	NS		10.7	10.7	0.0					2.7
	NNS		8.3	0.0	16.7					3.1

Refusal	Downgraders	9 +++	10 ++-	11 +-+	12 +--	13 -++	14 -+-	15 --+	16 ---	High Use Average
PoliteMark	NS	7.1								0.9
	NNS	16.7								2.1
Subjunctive	NS		3.6		7.1					1.3
	NNS		16.7		16.7					4.2
Hedge	NS		14.3							1.8
	NNS		0.0							0.0
Understate	NS			0.0						0.0
	NNS			16.7						2.1
Appealer	NS		10.7							1.3
	NNS		8.3							1.0

Apology	Downgraders	17 +++	18 ++-	19 +-+	20 +--	21 -++	22 -+-	23 --+	24 ---	High Use Average
Downtoner	NS			10.7	10.7					2.7
	NNS			0.0	8.3					1.0
Pause Filler	NS				14.3					1.8
	NNS				8.3					1.0
Subjunctive	NS				7.1					0.9
	NNS				8.3					1.0

apologies were 3.1% for NSs and 2.1% for NNSs. However, NNSs did show dominance on request cell 8 (NNSs 25.0%, NSs 14.3%), and similar use compared to NSs on apology cell 20 (NNSs 8.3%, NSs 10.7%). *Pause fillers* were used on +R request cells 1, 3, and 4 with NNS dominance (NNSs 16.7%, 16.7%, 25.0%, and NSs 0%, 3.6%, 3.6% respectively), and on apology cell 20 with NS dominance (NSs 14.3%, 8.3%). The great difference between NS and NNS use of this strategy in requests is shown in Table 17 (NNS 9.4%, NS 0.9%). Greater use of *pause fillers* in requests on the part of NNS may either show a lack of confidence in request realization or be the result of transfer. *Subjunctive* showed use across various +R request, refusal, and apology cells, with similar NS and NNS use on cells 1 (NSs 10.7%, NNSs 16.7%) and 20 (NSs 7.1%, NNSs 8.3%), and NNS dominance on cells 10 and 12 (NNSs 16.7% and 16.7%, and NSs 3.6% and 7.1% respectively). *Hedge* had isolated use on refusal cell 10 with NS dominance (NSs 14.3%, NNSs 0%). *Understater* had isolated use on request cell 8 with great NS dominance (NSs 21.4%, NNSs 0%), and refusal cell 10 with NNS dominance (NNSs 16.7%, NSs 0%). *Appealer* was used only on refusal cell 10 with similar use by NSs and NNSs, 10.7% and 8.3%, respectively. Most of the request only downgraders had low use. *Aspect and tense* were used on +R cells 2, 3, and 4, with NNS dominance on cells 2 and 4, and fairly equal use on cell 3. Overall differences between NS and NNS use of aspect on requests is noteworthy (NNS 10.4%, NS 4.5%), as shown in Table 16. Again, this difference shows a level of NNS tentativeness in request realization. *Conditional clause* was also used on cells 2 through 4: similar use occurred on cell 2 (NSs 10.7%, NNSs 8.3%); NSs dominated on cell 3 (NSs 10.7%, NNSs 0%); and NNS dominance was shown on cell 4 (NNSs 16.7%, NSs 0%).

To conclude, for requests, it seems that NSs and NNSs agreed on which cells to downgrade. However, they often used different strategies with which to realize such downgrading. For refusals, NSs and NNSs showed varying agreement on the use of downgrader strategies for specific cells. For apologies, while only NSs downgraded cell 19, both groups agreed that cell 20 required downgrading, and they tended to realize it in the same way.

Upgraders. Among the upgrader strategies, *intensifiers*, *emotion*, and *emphasis* were more highly used than *lexical upgraders* and *expletives*, with overall NS and NNS averages from 23.2% to 5.6% (see Table 18).

Intensifiers were used on all +R cells, across all speech acts. NS and NNS use proved similar on requests (NSs 14.3%, NNSs 15.6%) and apologies (30.8%, NNSs 33.3%), as shown in Table 18. However, for refusals, since NNSs limited their use of *intensifiers* to the +R cells 9, 10, and 11, NS use exceeded NNS use with averages of 24.6% and 16.7% respectively. Overall use for NSs was 23.2%, and for NNSs was 21.9%. In general, the NSs appear to have perceived the –R cells of refusals and apologies as more deserving of intensification than the NNSs did. *Emotion* was used heavily for apologies (excluding +R/–D cells), with overall average use of 29.5% for NSs and 39.6% for NNSs. NNS use predominated across all speech act cells except refusal cell 11 (NSs 32.1%, NNSs 8.3%). Use for refusals fell mainly on +R cells, with similar overall averages of 12.9% for NSs and 13.5% for NNSs. The only use of emotion for request cells was by NNSs, at 16.7% in cell 8. Use of *emphasis* was dominated by NSs across all speech acts (overall averages, NSs 13.4%, NNSs 5.6%) but fell mainly on the apology cells (NSs 29.0%, NNSs 13.5%) where NSs dominated on cells 17, 18, and 22–24. Here again, NSs apparently found the speech act of apology more deserving of upgrading than the NNSs did.

Table 18: Averages of upgrader use overall and by speech act

Alerter Strategy	Total Average	NS/NNS Breakdown		Speech Act		
				Request	Refusal	Apology
Intensifier	45.1	NS	23.2	14.3	24.6	30.8
		NNS	21.9	15.6	16.7	33.3
Emotion	33.7	NS	15.3	3.6	12.9	29.5
		NNS	18.4	2.1	13.5	39.6
Emphasis	18.9	NS	13.4	6.7	4.5	29.0
		NNS	5.6	2.1	1.0	13.5
Lexical Up	6.7	NS	3.3	3.1	3.1	3.6
		NNS	3.5	6.3	2.1	2.1
Expletive	0.6	NS	0.6	0.0	0.0	1.8
		NNS	0.0	0.0	0.0	0.0

Minimal or Sporadic Use Upgraders. In addition to the use of *emphasis* in apologies, as described above, NS and NNS used *emphasis* sporadically in request cell 2 (NSs 21.4%, NNSs 16.7%). NSs also used it in request cell 4 (10.7%) and refusal cells 11 and 15 (10.7% each). The use of *lexical upgraders* was limited to request cell 3 (NSs at 14.3%, and NNSs at a high 41.7%), refusal cells 9 (NSs 10.7%, NNSs 8.3%) and 10 (NSs 10.7%, NNSs 0%), and apology cells 18 (NSs 17.9%, NNSs 8.3%) and 19 (NSs 10.7%, NNSs 8.3%). All of these cells are +R cells. The use of *expletives* always demonstrated limited to low use, so is not i ncluded in

Table 19: Use of *upgraders* by cell for requests, refusals and apologies

Strategies		Use by Cell with R, P, and D Designations								High Use
Request Upgraders		1 +++	2 ++-	3 +-+	4 +--	5 -++	6 -+-	7 --+	8 ---	Average
Intensifier	NS	32.1	7.1	46.4	28.6					14.3
	NNS	16.7	25.0	58.3	25.0					15.6
Emotion	NS								0.0	0.0
	NNS								16.7	2.1
Emphasis	NS		21.4		10.7					4.0
	NNS		16.7		0.0					2.1
Lexical Up	NS			14.3						1.8
	NNS			41.7						5.2
Refusal Upgraders		9 +++	10 ++-	11 +-+	12 +--	13 -++	14 -+-	15 --+	16 ---	High Use Average
Intensifier	NS	42.9	67.9	28.6	32.1	10.7	53.6	10.7		30.8
	NNS	16.7	33.3	25.0	0.0	0.0	0.0	0.0		9.4
Emotion	NS	3.6	10.7	32.1	7.1	7.1	14.3		21.4	12.1
	NNS	16.7	16.7	8.3	16.7	8.3	16.7		25.0	13.5
Emphasis	NS			10.7				10.7		2.7
	NNS			0.0				0.0		0.0
Lexical Up	NS	10.7	10.7							2.7
	NNS	8.3	0.0							1.0

Apology Upgraders		17 +++	18 ++-	19 +-+	20 +--	21 -++	22 -+-	23 --+	24 ---	High Use Average
Intensifier	NS	78.6	75.0	64.3	10.7	3.6	14.3			30.8
	NNS	50.0	83.3	66.7	41.7	8.3	0.0			31.3
Emotion	NS	75.0		35.7		32.1	53.6	21.4	17.9	29.5
	NNS	83.3		41.7		66.7	58.3	33.3	33.3	39.6
Emphasis	NS	53.6	14.3	39.3			53.6	35.7	25.0	27.7
	NNS	33.3	0.0	41.7			16.7	16.7	0.0	13.5
Lexical Up	NS		17.9	10.7						3.6
	NNS		8.3	8.3						2.1

the tables. However, note that although it had low use by NSs on apology cells 17, 18, and 22, it was never used by NNSs.

To conclude, use of upgraders by NSs and NNSs shows a willingness by both groups to add upgraders to their realizations. Nonetheless, NNS use of upgraders on certain cells did not reach the levels shown by the NSs. This difference in emotional expressiveness may be due to transfer from Japanese culture.

Miscellaneous Strategies. *Opt out*, coded when NSs or NNSs did not carry out the intended speech act, had isolated use on refusal cell 13 with NS dominance (NSs 14.3%, NNSs 0%). Not surprisingly, NNSs dominated on the non-strategy of *non-code*, which was used for strategies that were essentially unrecognizable. *Non-code* was found in request cell 1 (NNSs 16.7%, NSs 3.6%), refusal cell 10 (NNSs 16.7%, NSs 0%), and apology cell 17 (NNSs 16.7%, NSs 3.6%), all +R/+P cells.

Summary of Strategies Common to All Three Speech Acts

Native speaker and non-native speaker trends in the overall use of strategies common to the three speech acts showed general similarities for the higher use strategies such as *attention getters, politeness markers, intensifiers,* and *emotion.* However, differences in strategy use between NSs and NNSs were found upon investigation of use by cell. These differences were particularly common for the lower use strategies and often seemed to be related to the power and distance designations.

Final Conclusion of Results

The results of NS and NNS speech act realizations across the three speech acts showed numerous similarities and various types of differences. First, in general, NSs and NNSs showed generally similar use of the more commonly used strategies. This trend was found for strategies both specific and common to the speech acts. Furthermore, the effect of the distinction between plus and minus degree of imposition on the realizations proved interesting for both the NSs and NNSs. Both groups used fewer strategies for the realization of –R situations, which, when comparing the groups, resulted in fairly similar responses on those cells.

In spite of the general trends of similarity discussed above, two systematic sets of differences between NS and NNS speech act realization were found in the data. First, pragmalinguistic differences were found in the data. NNSs realizations of strategy types included numerous linguistic moves that made them characteristically non-native. Second, linguistic differences resulting from the plus and minus distinctions for power and distance were found. Most of these differences were related to power. NNSs, being in roles of plus or minus power, performed in ways categorically different from the NSs. Differences took the form of both number and type of strategies used, so that in some cases, the NNSs were using a strategy to a different degree than the NSs, and in other cases they were using strategies completely foreign to the NS realizations. Thus, the data showed how sociopragmatic judgment affects NNS speech act realization.

The results of the analysis show the subjects performing as one would expect NSs and NNSs would. At times, they showed very similar language use, and at other times their use differed both pragmalinguistically and sociopragmatically.

DCT Version #3

Based on the analysis of item performance on DCT Version #2, the DCT was revised slightly. DCT Version #3 is very similar to Version #2. Small revisions were made after further consideration of the items while working on the multiple-choice version of the DCT discussed below (See Appendix E for DCT Version #3). DCT Version #3 appears to be the final version of the open-ended DCT format. Hence, this version is now ready to be administered to a large sample of NSs and NNSs for analysis.

RATING SUBJECT PERFORMANCE ON THE DCT

In the proposed system, the evaluation of NNS performance on the DCT will involve ratings by trained NSs of the NNS responses or utterances on six aspects of pragmatic competence using a five-point rating scale ranging from very unsatisfactory at (1) to completely appropriate at (5). The intermediate points, 2 through 4, do not include verbal labels. The decision to have a five-point scale was influenced by the literature review of self-assessment which is discussed in the following section. The six aspects of pragmatic competence were decided upon after reviewing the literature as discussed in Hudson, Detmer, and Brown, 1992. The six aspects of pragmatic competence include the ability to use the correct speech act, typical expressions, amount of speech and information, and levels of formality, directness, and politeness.

Ability to Use the Correct Speech Act

Since each situation was designed to elicit a particular speech act, the NS raters consider and rate the degree to which each response captures what they consider to be the speech act the situation was intended to elicit. However, the three speech acts are not mutually exclusive. For example, a request might begin with an apology: "I'm sorry, but could you move your car?"

This response is still a request. As long as the response includes the speech act within it, it should be considered appropriate and rated accordingly by the NSs. It may also be the case that the response given is very indirect or is intended to introduce a topic without actually getting to the point. In these cases, raters will still rate the given response on its appropriateness in the situation.

Typical Expressions

This category includes use of typical speech or gambits. Non-typical speech might be due to non-native speaker ignorance of a particular English phrase or due to some type of L2 transfer. Use of non-typical expressions was not uncommon in the DCT Version #2 NNS responses. In general, the raters' NS intuitions should serve them well in rating expressions. Note also that grammaticality is not considered an issue for our purposes. Both NNS and NS responses to the DCT Version #2 were found to contain grammatical errors in verb conjugation and article use.

Amount of Speech Used and Information Given

Speakers of any language adjust the amount of speech in a given speech act to fit the particular situation. For example, when making a request, speakers often include an explanation for the request. It has been hypothesized that when a non-native speaker uses more speech than the average native speaker, it is due to either elaboration or circumlocution often depending upon the speakers level of proficiency. Of course, a non-native speaker of lower proficiency might use very direct speech and thus produce an utterance which is shorter than the average NS utterance.

However, all variation in utterance length is not due to the speaker's level language proficiency. There is a degree of individual choice involved in how much one decides to say. Deciding how much speech and/or information is appropriate for a given situation might prove difficult for the raters because some individual variation is normal. As a guideline, raters are advised to use their NS intuition to judge when a response seems particularly abrupt or seems to provide too much unnecessary information.

Levels of Formality, Directness, and Politeness

These three distinct yet often overlapping elements of speech have been the subject of a great deal of discussion and research in pragmatics. While rating each response, raters are asked to try to keep these three concepts as distinct in their minds as possible, as discussed below.

Formality can be expressed through word choice, phrasing, use of titles, and choice of verb forms. Use of colloquial speech can be appropriate in

American English when the situation is informal and between friends, family, and co-workers. Yet here, too, a degree of appropriateness can apply. The NSs are the judges.

Pragmatically defined, most speech is indirect. However, raters are to rate the appropriateness of the level of *directness* found in the responses. Directness can be indicated by verb form or strategy choice. For example, the utterance "Would you mind passing the rice?" is less direct than "Pass me the rice" due to the verb form used. However, the statement "It's hot in here" is a different request strategy type and is less direct than the statement "Could you open the window?".

Politeness has many dimensions and has been the topic of numerous discussions in speech act studies. Politeness includes the aspects of formality and directness, among other aspects such as the strategy of politeness markers (for example, "please" and "thank you"). Due to its many elements, it is virtually impossible to prescribe a formula of politeness to any given situation. For example, NSs of English might use first names in a job situation, but it is not necessarily inappropriate to use Mr., Ms., or Mrs. with a surname on the job. Furthermore, if one combines the use of first names with politeness markers in a work situation, the utterance as a whole might be seen as appropriately polite.

A training manual was written for the NS raters (see Appendix J) and is ready to be piloted. The manual defines and explains the six aspects of pragmatic competence described above, providing criteria for rating and tips on trouble-shooting, and concludes with examples and a sample rating sheet. Note that the raters, when judging the appropriateness of the amount of information given and the levels of formality, directness and politeness, are to first give their ratings using the five point scale. After this, in the case of low ratings (1's and 2's), raters are to indicate if they think the response is inappropriate due to a greater or lesser degree of the aspect in question. For example, if a NS is rating a response and thinks it is far too long, he or she should give a rating of (1) and then circle the (+) sign to indicate that it is inappropriate because it is too long. This process allows the researchers a better understanding of NS reactions to NNS realizations. During the training session, all of the information in the manual will be discussed and the raters will work through the three examples with the trainer.

ON-GOING DCT ISSUES

The identification of NS/NNS differences will be utilized in three ways. First, the differences revealed between the NS and the NNS realizations, such as those just outlined, can give a good indication of just how "correctly" or "incorrectly" the NNS are performing on a given cell. These differences have been examined in the process of developing distractors for the multiple-choice cued response DCT. Secondly, depending on how the relationship of NSs and NNSs on –R items in future administrations of the DCT develop, in English and in other languages, the –R cells might warrant being eliminated from the design of the instruments. In other words, if the NNSs consistently perform very similarly to NSs on –R items, the items might be deleted in order to save test-taker and researcher resources. Third, some situations designed for the same cell elicit different strategies. When sufficient responses are obtained in the next phase of the project, it will be easier to code the strategies particular to a cell rather than a situation. This issue will be examined in revisions of the tests. For example, it is inherent in apologies that they are post event, whereas requests are pre-event. However, apologies may be immediately post event or there may be a period of time between the event and the need to apologize. Such differences will need to be examined systematically in order to determine the effect of such variables as they delimit each cell.

Cued Multiple-Choice DCT

The multiple-choice DCT item situations and cell designations are identical to the three forms of DCT Version #3. Several steps were involved in determining the format as well as the specifications of the answers and distractors for the multiple-choice forms before the final format was decided upon and written. This process is described below.

Initially, it was thought that the multiple-choice answers and distractors could be based directly on the results of the analysis of DCT Version #2 NS and NNS strategy use by cell. In this way, multiple-choice answers and distractors would have coincided directly with the most frequently used strategies used by each group for a particular cell. An attempt was made to select NS and NNS responses from the DCT Version #2 data to fit these criteria. The decisions about which strategies to use for a given cell were to be made following an established framework. In the framework, strategies would be considered and compared against the other strategies of the same type. For example, the strategy of first name falls under the type of alerter. The decision to use first names in either the answer or distractor for a multiple-choice item of a given cell would first involve comparing the use of first names to other alerter strategies used in that cell.

The comparison of NS and NNS strategies within a type was broken down according to a number of considerations. First, within a type, if there was different high-use strategies for the NSs and the NNSs, and similar use for the other strategies, the conflicting strategies were to be used, with the NNS strategy as the distractor. Second, within a type, if one group used only one strategy and the other group did not use a strategy from this type, then the strategy used would become either the distractor (if NNSs used it) or the non-use would become the distractor (if NSs used it). Third, within a type, if there was very high use on a strategy and low use on the other strategies for both NSs and NNSs, then the high use strategy was to be used in both the answer and the distractors. Thus, no distractors would be generated from that type. Fourth, within a type, if there was a very high-use strategy and conflicting NS and NNS use on two other lesser-used strategies, then the lesser-used strategies were to be used, with the NNS strategy as the distractor. However, a problems arose in those instances in which the percentage of use of the higher-NS-use strategy was in fact less than the NS use of the higher-NNS-use strategy — in other words, with a strategy that was used by NSs more than NNSs, but was not actually their first choice strategy. Fifth, within a type, if NS and NNS performance was very similar, a number of issues needed to be considered: 1) if a strategy within a type had very high use, its inclusion would be necessary in order to make the item sound natural; 2) if a strategy within a type specific to a speech act had very high use, its inclusion would be necessary in order to make the item comprehensible; 3) if all strategies within a common type had low (and equal) use, no strategies from this type were included.

Hence using the initially proposed framework frequently was problematic. First, the strategies with the highest use might not necessarily be used in combination with each other. For example, as in the requests, although the preparator and the intensifier had high use within their types, it was possible that they never occurred together in a response. Second, the results of the DCT analysis did not distinguish between the three specific situations on the three forms. So, a strategy may have been very appropriate for a given situation on Form A, but not at all appropriate for the corresponding situation on Form B. Another problem that revealed itself in this analysis and throughout the development of the multiple-choice forms, was that for some cells even the NNS responses that were chosen as distractors because they best represented the established criteria, although uncommonly used by NS, did not seem strange or obviously pragmatically incorrect for the situation.

In spite of the problems discussed above, the format decided upon was a standard multiple-choice format of one answer and two distractors per item (for item specifications see Appendix F). However, decisions about what made up the correct answers and the distractors were based on a method other than the one initially proposed. For the answers, NS responses to DCT Version #2 were studied to find the most typical NS response(s) for the specific situation. In some cases, it was necessary to modify a response or to create a composite version of a few NS responses, thus representing a typical NS response. NS and NNS responses to DCT Version #2 were studied in order to determine relevant criteria for distractor construction for given cells and items. Differences in strategy use, degree of directness, politeness and formality, and amount of information and length were studied. Trends in use were found for each speech act. For *requests*, NNSs seemed to have much less difficulty with the –R items. Nonetheless, NNS responses often tended to be too direct compared to NSs on the all of the –P cells, including those that were –R (7 and 8, –R; and 3 and 4, +R). The main problem NNSs had with *refusals* was also due to incorrect levels of directness, a problem in all cells except #10. Here, too, the NNSs tended to be more direct than the NS. The +R cells opened up more opportunity for distinct differences, which took the form of various strategy uses on all of the +R cells. Due to the nature of the speech act, the directness factor for the *apology* responses was often difficult to determine, particularly with the –R cells. Rather, the main issue for apology responses was the use of strategies, those that seemed incorrect or very odd compared to NS norms. *Offer of repair* and *concern for hearer* strategies were those most often misused by the NNSs. Based on the above trends, an overall framework was established to judge how NNS choices differed from NS choices across all cells according to the speech acts and the specific P, D, and R values (see Table 20). Distractors were then chosen from real NNS responses, fitting the overall system, and thus allowing the three forms to be parallel. For a number of situations, the NNS responses had to be modified to fit the framework. Such modifications allowed for significantly greater consistency across both the forms and the cells. Nonetheless, in some cases, due to differences inherent in the individual situations, it was difficult or impossible to make all three of the forms parallel.

The answers and distractors were edited numerous times. For many items, the distractors had to be modified due to their not being clearly incorrect from a pragmatic perspective. Data are presently being collected. Until they are analyzed, the effectiveness of the distractors will be difficult to determine. For a final draft of the multiple-choice forms, see Appendix G.

Table 20: Multiple-choice Version #1, answer and distractor key

Situation 1	Situation 2	Situation 3	Situation 4
a) short b) NS c) strategy	a) strategy b) direct c) NS	a) NS b) indirect c) direct	a) NS b) formal c) direct
Situation 5	**Situation 6**	**Situation 7**	**Situation 8**
a) direct b) indirect c) NS	a) direct b) NS c) strategy	a) NS b) direct c) strategy	a) strategy b) direct c) NS
Situation 9	**Situation 10**	**Situation 11**	**Situation 12**
a) NS b) direct c) strategy	a) strategy b) NS c) direct	a) NS b) formal c) strategy	a) NS b) direct c) polite
Situation 13	**Situation 14**	**Situation 15**	**Situation 16**
a) strategy b) NS c) direct	a) indirect b) short c) NS	a) NS b) strategy c) direct	a) indirect b) NS c) polite
Situation 17	**Situation 18**	**Situation 19**	**Situation 20**
a) direct b) strategy c) NS	a) strategy b) strategy c) NS	a) strategy b) NS c) short	a) NS b) direct c) strategy
Situation 21	**Situation 22**	**Situation 23**	**Situation 24**
a) direct b) strategy c) NS	a) strategy b) NS c) direct	a) strategy b) NS c) misc.	a) strategy b) direct c) NS

DEVELOPMENT OF THE ORAL-AURAL INSTRUMENTS

LISTENING LAB

The development of the listening lab instrument involved the direct transfer of situations from DCT Version #3 (see Appendix H). Whereas in the paper and pencil DCT versions subjects read the situations and wrote their responses, in the listening lab version, subjects read silently along with a provided oral reading of the situations and then respond to the situations orally. Subject responses are audiotaped. The listening lab version has not yet been piloted. After initial data are collected, the results will be compared to the written DCT results. The examinee results will also be rated on the five point rating scale used to rate the open-ended DCT responses.

Development of the Structured Interview

In developing the structured oral interview to assess cross-cultural pragmatics, two areas had to be addressed. First, it was essential to determine the appropriate format of the oral assessment. Second, it was necessary to examine the role of performance assessment in education and business. These areas are of central concern because the assessment procedure of the present study must elicit a sample of the speech acts of request, refusal, or apology. As such, it differs from more traditional oral interviews that focus on a language sample that is to be evaluated for grammatical and phonological accuracy or fluency.

Appropriate Oral Assessment Format

A number of interview formats have been utilized over the past several years. Heaton (1988), for example, describes five formats for oral testing. The formats include: 1) oral grammar drills; 2) short situational role-plays; 3) free student response to stimulus, for example a student might hear "May I borrow your pencil?" and respond with whatever he or she thinks is appropriate; 4) dialogues "for the deaf" where students respond to a number of stimuli that, no matter how they respond, follow a set course; and finally, 5) incomplete dialogues where the student "interacts" with one person in a roleplay while receiving cues from another person "whispered in the ear". Although some of the formats were of interest and served as a springboard for a number of future ideas, it was decided that the more conventional situational roleplay format was the best choice. A survey of foreign language departments carried out by Harlow and Caminero (1990) revealed that within the departments that did oral interview testing, 55% of the tests had a roleplay component. This study provided further support for the decision to use roleplays in the structured interview.

Several issues arose regarding the development and implementation of the roleplay. First there was the issue of the design of the interview. Eckard and Kearney (1981) define roleplay as "a type of skit in which learners assume the identity of individual characters in a given situation and engage in a conversation that reflects the personalities, needs, and desires of the characters they are asked to portray.... The emphasis is on the verbal interchanges rather than on the actions" (p. 20). Thus, it is important to design situations where the action does not tend to eclipse the desired oral exchange. Second, Ur (1981) raises another key issue in roleplay design; it is not primarily what you are talking about that is most important, but why. Content and purpose are crucial to successful roleplay. When writing roleplays, the objective must be clearly specified so that interlocutors know that they are talking about X in situation Y in order to achieve Z. Thus, all of the roleplays developed for the current project include an objective that is highlighted to the interlocutors involved in the described situation. Furthermore, Dougill (1987) points out the importance of conflict and tension in drama and applies its importance to roleplay situations. Dougill thinks that classroom roleplays tend to lack the excitement of "true" drama because of the lack of conflict and unpredictability. Dougill writes, "if participants know what the others are going to say there can be little chance of anything but the mere exchange of words" (pp. 18–19). In order to make the roleplay situations meaningful, an effort was made to include a degree of unpredictability in each one. For example, a number of the scenarios are split into two parts so that the subjects, once they begin the roleplay, encounter the unexpected. Finally, Donahue and Parsons (1982) and Eckard and Kearney (1981) provided some guidelines on roleplay procedure. They stress demonstrations and practice to allow players an opportunity to increase comfort and confidence. These components were also included in our format.

Role of Performance Assessment

There has been an increasing focus on performance assessment in education and business. Frechtling (1991) explains that although performance assessment has been used in U.S. public schools for years, it has currently reached fad status. Although she seems to support its use, she points out that it is time-consuming, difficult to objectively judge, and costly to develop. The use of performance assessment is also being developed in business and industry as a tool for hiring decisions. Costentino, Allen, and Wellins (1990) describe the hiring process for a new Toyota plant in Georgetown, KY., which includes Interpersonal Skills Performance Assessment (ISPA) at an assessment center. During ISPA, prospective employees engage in four simulations taking eight hours. Due to the high price of ISPA at formal assessment centers, some companies are opting for a more generic video version of performance assessment. As described by Fisher (1992), applicants are given a computer-generated composite score after viewing 27 different scenarios and choosing from four courses of action, a kind of video multiple-choice format. However, in order to obtain a speech sample representing the performance of a request, refusal, or apology, the present assessment program rejected the multiple-choice approach in favor of roleplay.

Development and Format of Roleplays

The 72 DCT situations, 24 each on Forms A, B, and C, were rewritten into a roleplay format. Through this process, a number of considerations revealed themselves, some of them parallel to those outlined in the literature review. First, the use of a person in addition to the interviewer is desirable for the performance of the roleplay scenario. Providing the second player ensures that the test taker does not allow the real life role of the interviewer to influence his or her performance in the roleplay scenarios. Hence the interviewer can focus his or her attention more fully on the task of setting up and explaining each scenario and on the audio or video taping of the scenarios. Second, the individual situations should not place too much of a burden on the test taker in terms of conceptualization and actualization of the scenario. Third, although the test taker is assuming a role, the test is not an acting test. Thus, the scenarios should keep the action involved in the roleplay to a minimum and not include highly dramatic elements. Fourth, it is necessary to consider how much of the roleplay involves action and how much involves language. Finally, the use of props, such as paper, pencils, or other small items involved in the situation, is helpful to the test taker if not used in excess. These issues, in addition to those raised in the literature reviews, were taken into consideration when transforming the original DCT situations into roleplay scenarios.

However, an interview containing 24 roleplay situations, as in the DCT, would clearly take far too long and place too much of a burden on the test taker. Thus, eight scenes were written, each containing a request, a refusal, and an apology. By balancing the level of power and the degree of distance and imposition across the eight scenes, all 24 cells were covered in the interview. Care was taken to follow the considerations discussed in the literature review and directly above. For example, in order to limit the degree of burden in terms of conceptualization and actualization on the part of the test taker, none of the scenes contained more than two speech acts with a high degree of imposition. The initial scenes were piloted on five NSs. Revisions were made after each NS piloting, so that some items went through a number of revisions, while others remained unchanged. The revisions were based on the speech acts produced by the NSs and on oral feed-back provided by the NSs after all eight roleplays were performed. For example, in one case, a number of the NSs failed to perform one of the three speech acts. Through discussion with the NSs, it became clear that the roleplay prompt was too involved and difficult to remember. Thus, it was broken into two parts. However, most of the revisions were based on NS comments about specific wording of the prompt, and involved providing more details. For example, for the job interview scene, a number of the players commented that a name for the office manager should be provided, rather than players having to invent the name on the spot. A number of other NS comments were regarding specificity of dates and times described in the situations. The NSs wanted specific days and times, rather than general descriptions such as "a few days later" or "later this evening". For a final version of the roleplay interview see Appendix H. Finally, after administering the interview to the five subjects and learning more about the actualization of each scenario, a guide providing cues for the speech and actions of the second player was written (see Appendix J). Each scene change or roleplay is written on a separate card that is kept by the interviewer. The interviewer provides a card to the interviewee at each scene change, whether that change is a new roleplay or an additional scene in an ongoing roleplay. Responses will be rated on the five point rating scale used in the open-ended DCT and the language laboratory DCT.

DEVELOPMENT OF SELF-ASSESSMENT FORMATS

THE THIRD METHOD OF CROSS-CULTURAL EVALUATION utilized in the present study involves self-assessment, an approach to assessment that has been gaining in interest recently. Two types of self-assessment were to be developed. The first was an instrument for the examinee to evaluate the extent to which he or she could succeed in one of the DCT situations. The second was an instrument for the examinee to rate his or her actual prior performance on the structured interview. A close examination of how previous self-assessment instruments perform may provide insight into the development of pre-screening devices.

Blanche (1988) undertook a review of the literature on self-assessment in the testing of foreign language skills of lower level language learners, and found that most studies showed Pearson product-moment correlations of .5 to .6 between students' self assessment ratings and external criteria. However, studies also indicate that if correlations are to be high, test takers require practice in taking self-assessment type tests (Oskarsson, 1980). The most accurate types of self-assessment items are those that "contain descriptions of concrete linguistic situations which the learner can size up in behavior terms" (Blanche, 1988, p. 81). Students who over-estimate their language ability tend to be lower level students. Furthermore, self-assessment is more accurate when learners assess their "purely communicative skills" rather than degree of proficiency in grammar or pronunciation. To conclude, studies of self assessment in language ability generally showed higher correlations than might be expected (Oskarsson, 1980, Von Elek, 1982, Davidson and Henning, 1985, and Bachman and Palmer, 1981).

Studies by Oskarsson (1980), Bachman and Palmer (1981), and Rea (1981) have shown "that adults are fully capable of making reliable judgments about their own mastery of a foreign language, provided they have adequate instruments" (Von Elek, 1985, p. 48). The development of adequate instruments is the basis for the discussion that follows.

DEVELOPMENT OF THE SELF-ASSESSMENT INSTRUMENT FOR ABILITY TO PERFORM IN SITUATIONS

In the development of the self-assessment instruments, numerous formats and question types used in self-assessment testing were evaluated. Oskarsson (1989) reviewed a variety of formats including progress cards, diaries, log books, informal self-assessment, video and audio cassettes, and questionnaires, rating scales, and check-lists. He concluded that questionnaires, rating scales, and check-lists were the most common. Bachman and Palmer (1989) conducted a study which employed three types of self-assessment questions: ability to use trait, "Do you use different types of English depending on the person you are using it with?"; recognition of input, "Can you tell how polite English speaking people are by the kind of English they use?"; difficulty in using trait, "How hard is it for you to organize a speech...?". They found the last question type, the difficulty in using trait question type, to be the most effective format. Thus, the present instrument adopted the trait question format.

LeBlanc and Painchaud (1985) reviewed various scales common to the questionnaire format. They point out that the kinds of questions asked in self-assessment instruments often influenced the type of scale used. Most consistently, however, scales have either 5 or 10 points. For example, in a study of graduate students in Thai universities by Wangsotorn (1980), a five-point scale was used with zero equal to "I do not speak English at all", three equal to "I can express myself, but with some difficulty", and five equal to "I can speak English as fluently as a native speaker of English" (p. 242).

The format of the self-assessment instruments is in many ways similar to the format used by the NS ratings of the NNS responses on the open-ended DCT and language laboratory DCT in that the NNSs read each situation and rate their intended performance on the same five-point scale. However, in this format, the subjects express their assessment through an overall rating. Thus, rather than breaking their ratings down into the six aspects of pragmatic competence, they give one rating while considering their general ability in the six aspects of pragmatic competence. See Appendix K for the Self Assessment instrument.

DEVELOPMENT OF THE SELF-ASSESSMENT
OF INTERVIEW PERFORMANCE

The second type of self-assessment developed in the present study was the subject's assessment of his or her performance on the structured interview. This self-assessment of the oral interview requires the subjects to rate their actual pragmatic performance. Here again the five-point scale is used. Further, the subjects rate their performance according to the six aspects of pragmatic ability used by the NS raters to rate NNS performance on the paper and pencil DCT and Language Lab DCT. Before viewing their performance on each scenario, however, some training will be provided. First, the intended speech acts will be reviewed. Then, the way that the rating sheets list the scenarios and order the speech acts will be discussed. Only then will the subjects follow along, watching the tape and marking their ratings on the sheet. See Appendix L for the instrument.

Bachman and Palmer (1982), in their multi-method study, tested subjects with the self-assessment method first to "prevent their responses from being influenced by their performance on the other tests" (p. 455). This issue is relevant to the present study in that it also intends to utilize a multi-method format. However, the ordering of the self-assessment relative to other tasks is also affected by the object of evaluation. In the present study, for example, since the self-assessment version of the DCT measures the subject's intended performance on the DCT instrument, it will be administered first, while since the self-assessment of the role-play version (discussed below) involves subjects rating their performance on the role-play, it will be administered last.

FUTURE DIRECTIONS

THIS REPORT HAS PRESENTED the steps taken in developing prototypes for instruments to assess cross-cultural pragmatics. It has presented these prototypes for paper and pencil formats, oral formats, and self-assessment formats. This variety of formats is proposed as an acknowledgment that different methods may be most effective for different speech acts and researcher purposes.

In the next phase of the project, steps will be taken to complete the analysis of the various instruments, administer the new forms to subjects, and develop Japanese and Korean versions of all of the instruments. First, in order to complete the analysis of the DCT #2 version, data already collected from lower level NNSs living in Japan will be analyzed. It is anticipated that, among Japanese, the speech act realizations of the EFL speakers will show trends different from those of the ESL speakers. Second, upon the collection and analysis of additional NS data on the multiple-choice forms, item analysis will be carried out and weak items will be revised. Then the revised multiple-choice forms will be administered and the results analyzed. Third, the listening lab, DCT self-evaluation, oral interview and interview performance self-evaluation instruments will be administered. The oral interview and self-evaluation of the oral interview instruments will be administered to subjects who have already been tested on all of the other instruments. Fourth, the rating manual will be revised and put into use. Finally, parallel versions of all of the instruments will be developed in Japanese and Korean in order to test the pragmatic competence of NNSs of Japanese and Koreans (in both J/KFL and J/KSL settings). These instruments will be administered, and the results will then be compared to the results found on the English versions.

Obviously, several issues remain to be resolved in the assessment of cross-cultural pragmatics. First, the role played by the "native speaker" as the standard against which performance is judged is far from resolved. Much more research will need to be conducted to address the variability of native speaker performance. Second, the decisions made on the basis of the results of assessment through the prototypic instruments must be carefully scrutinized. The instruments developed thus far in the present project are very preliminary suggestions for the forms that assessment might take. Thus, the instruments should be used for research purposes only, and no examinee level decisions should be made. Further validation studies are needed before we can be sure with any certainty what the results of the tests mean◆

REFERENCES

Bachman, L. (1990). *Fundamental considerations in language testing.* Oxford: Oxford University Press.

Bachman, L. & Palmer, A. (1982). The construct validation of some components of communicative proficiency. *TESOL Quarterly* 16, 449–466.

Bachman, L. & Palmer, A. (1981). A multitrait-multimethod investigation into the construct validity of six tests of speaking and reading. In A. Palmer, P. J. M. Groot, & G. A. Trosper (Eds.) *The Construct Validation of Tests of Communicative Competence* (pp. 149–165). Washington: TESOL.

Bachman, L. & Palmer, A. (1989). The construct validity of self-ratings of communicative language ability. *Language Testing* 6:15–29.

Beebe, L., Takahashi, T., & Uliss-Weltz, R. (1990). Pragmatic transfer in ESL refusals. In R. C. Scarcella, E. S. Andersen, & S. D. Krashen, (Eds.) *On the development of communicative competence in a second language.* New York: Newbury House. 55–74.

Blanche, P. (1988). Self-assessment of foreign language skills: Implications for teachers and researchers. *RELC Journal* 19 (1): 75–96.

Blum-Kulka, S. (1982). Learning to say what you mean in a second language: A study of speech act performance of learners of Hebrew as a second language. *Applied Linguistics* 3:29–59.

Blum-Kulka, S. (1987a). Lexical and grammatical pragmatic indicators. *Studies in Second Language Acquisition* 9:155–170.

Blum-Kulka, S. (1987b). Indirectness and politeness in requests: Same or different? *Journal of Pragmatics* 11:131–146.

Blum-Kulka, S., House, J., & Kasper, G., (Eds.). (1989). *Cross-cultural pragmatics: Requests and apologies.* Norwood, NJ.: Ablex Publishing Company.

Borland International Inc. (1987). *Quatro Pro 4.0.* [Computer program]. Scotts Valley, CA: Borland.

Brown, P. & Levinson, D. (1987). *Politeness: Some universals in language usage.* Cambridge: Cambridge University Press.

Canale, M. (1988). The measurement of communicative competence. *Annual Review of Applied Linguistics* 8:67–84.

Canale, M. & Swain, M. (1980). Theoretical bases of communicative approaches to second language teaching and testing. *Applied Linguistics* 1:1–47.

Costentino, C., Allen, J., & Wellins, R. (1990). Choosing the right people. *HR Magazine* 35 (3): 66–70.

Davidson, F. & Henning, G. (1985). A self-rating scale of English difficulty. *Language Testing* 2: 164–179.

Donahue, M. & Parsons, A. H. (1982). The use of roleplay to overcome cultural fatigue. *TESOL Quarterly* 16 (3): 359–365.

Dougill, J. (1987). *Drama activities for language learning.* London: Macmillan.

Eckard, R. & Kearny, M. A. (1981). Teaching conversation skills in ESL. *Language in education: Theory and practice*, 38. Washington, D. C.: Center for Applied Linguistics.

Fisher, R. (1992). Screen test. *Canadian Business* 65 (5): 62– 64.

Fraser, B. (1990) Perspectives on politeness. *Journal of Pragmatics* 14: 219–236.

Frechtling, J. A. (1991). Performance assessment: Moonstruck or the real thing? *Educational Measurement: Issues and Practice* 10 (1): 23–25.

Harlow, L. & Caminero, R. (1990). Oral testing of beginning language students at large universities: Is it worth the trouble? *Foreign Language Annals* 23 (6): 489–499.

Heaton, J. B. (1988). *Writing English language tests.* Longman.

Hudson, T., Detmer, E., & Brown, J. D. (1992). *A framework for testing cross-cultural pragmatics.* Technical Report (2). Honolulu: Second Language Teaching and Curriculum Center, University of Hawai'i at Mānoa.

Kasper, G. & Dahl, M. (1991). *Research methods in interlanguage pragmatics.* Technical Report (1). Honolulu: Second Language Teaching and Curriculum Center, University of Hawai'i at Mānoa.

LeBlanc, R. & Painchaud, G. (1985). Self-assessment as a second language placement instrument. *TESOL Quarterly* 19 (4): 673–687.

MacWhinney, B. (1991). *The CHILDES Project: Tools for analyzing talk.* Hillsdale, N. J.: Lawrence Erlbaum Associates.

Norusis, M. J. (1988). *SPSS/PC+ v2.0.* [Computer program]. Chicago: SPSS, Inc.

Oskarsson, M. (1980). *Approaches to self-assessment in foreign language learning.* Oxford: Pergamon Press.

Oskarsson, M. (1989). Self-assessment of language proficiency: Rationale and applications. *Language Testing* 6 (1): 1–13.

Popham, W. J. (1978). *Criterion-Referenced Measurement.* Englewood Cliffs: Prentice Hall.

Rea, P. M. (1981). Formative assessment of student performance: The role of self-appraisal. *Indian Journal of Applied Linguistics* 7 (1): 66–88.

Ur, P. (1981). *Discussions that work: Task-centered fluency practice.* Cambridge: Cambridge University Press.

Von Elek, T. (1982). *Test of Swedish as a second language: An experiment in self-assessment.* Goteborg: Goteborgs Universitet, Sprakpedagogiskt Centrum.

Von Elek, T. (1985). A test of Swedish as a second language: An experiment in self-assessment. In Y. P. Lee, C. Y. Y. Fok, R. Lord, & G. Low (Eds.) *New Directions in Language Testing.* Oxford: Pergamon.

Wangsotorn, A. (1980). Self-assessment in English skills by undergraduate and graduate students in Thai universities. In J. A. S. Read (Ed.) *Directions in Language Testing, Selected papers from RELC Seminar.* Singapore: Singapore University Press.

APPENDICES

APPENDIX A: ITEM SPECIFICATIONS FOR OPEN-ENDED DCT

General Description

Given a short description of a situation which elicits either a request, refusal or apology, the examinees will write what they think they would say in a given situation.

Sample Item

Directions: Read each of the situations on the following pages. After each situation write what you would say in the situation in a normal conversation. The situations take place in the United States and are to be answered in English.

Example:

Situation: You live in a large apartment building. You are leaving to go to work. On your way out, you meet your next door neighbor, whom you haven't seen for a long time.

You: _____
_____
_____

Prompt Attribute

The situation and dialogue are specifically designed to elicit either a request, refusal or an apology.

The prompt includes a short description of the given situation and an incomplete dialogue. The description and dialogue serve to define the context of the situation and include information about the roles of the speakers including: power relationship, distance between the two speakers, and the degree of imposition involved in the speech act. See attached variable parameters .

Constraints on Prompt Construction

1.   Neither interlocutor has gender specified.
2.   Situation must be face to face. No situation can be over the telephone or written.

3. For requests, the explicit statement beginning with either "You want..." or "You need..." must be used in the prompt.
4. Situation is context internal to the roles. For example, if the roles of the interlocutors are "project leader" to "project worker", the context of the speech event is at work and has to do with work related activities.
5. No explicit money is to be involved in the contexts.
6. No contexts for apologies are due to physical contact, injury or violating social norms.
7. For designation of power relationships with minus social distance (in-group), formal explicit relationships should be designated when possible (e.g., president of a chapter of a national hiking club, group leader, department head, etc.).
8. No socially stigmatized roles should be included (e.g., rich patron—maid, etc.).
9. Avoid professionally defined or formulaic interactional patterns (e.g., doctor—patient, lawyer—client, patron—ticket seller, requests for the time of day, etc.).
10. No relationships with family, friends, enemies or intimates should be included.
11. Situations will be familiar to examinees.

Response Attributes

As discussed above, the prompts are designed to elicit a specific speech act (request, refusal, apology). Responses will be broken down into their components according to established coding scales and analyzed through comparison to responses of native speakers.

OR

Responses will be coded (according to established scales), analyzed and collapsed into a form to be judged by native speakers in terms of their acceptability. Based on the ratings by the NS, the response-types will be assigned values.

Responses will not be judged in terms of their grammaticality except in cases where it is determined to cause a breakdown of communication.

APPENDIX B: EXAMPLE NS RATING PROBLEMS

Problem Items: Speech Act
(Some situations required more than one speech act)

Item 3, Form A: Supposed to be Request; 3 NSs thought Apology.

> You work in a computer store as a salesperson. Last week
> you were sick and had to reschedule all of your sales
> appointments. You have an appointment with a customer for
> 1:30 today, but you discover that you have an appointment
> with your dentist and won't return until 4:00. It's one
> o'clock and your customer has just arrived.
>
> You: _____
> _____
> _____
>
> Customer: Oh, I understand. I can come back at 4:00.

Item 9, Form A: Supposed to be Refusal; 4 NSs thought Request.

> You work in a large company. You and a group of your co-
> workers are working on a special project. Your boss has
> put you in charge of the group. Last week you assigned
> part of the project to another person in the group and
> asked to have it finished by tomorrow. Your Co-worker
> comes into your office and asks for more time to finish
> it. You need this part of the project for a meeting with
> the boss tomorrow.
>
> You: _____
> _____
> _____
>
> Co-worker: Okay. Well, I'll have it finished tomorrow
> then.

Problem Items: Power Relationships
(Tended to be problematic when Distance was –D)

Item 20, Form A: Supposed to be +P; 3 NSs thought –P.

> You are president of a student organization. You see a
> member of the organization in the student center. The

member knows that you have a class with a fellow student this afternoon. You are not going to that class this afternoon because you have a doctor's appointment.

You: _____
_____
_____

Member: Okay. Well, I'll try to go to the class myself. Thanks anyway.

Item 1, Form B: Supposed to be +P; 2 NSs thought –P.

You are president of a student organization. You have a meeting with another member of the organization at two o'clock at the student center. You are a few minutes late for the meeting. You arrive at the student center and see that the member is waiting.

You: _____
_____
_____

Member: It's okay, I had some reading to do.

Problem Items: Distance
(Instances when we evaluated as +D and NSs evaluated as –D)

Item 23, Form A: Supposed to be +D; 2 NSs thought –D.

Last night you tried on the clothes you plan to wear to a wedding tomorrow night. However, you discovered that the clothes are too large for you now. Today you go to a small tailor shop that your family has used for years. You want them to do a rush job for you, but you know they are very busy.

You: _____
_____
_____

Clerk: I think I can have it ready for you by four o'clock tomorrow afternoon.

Problem Items: Degree of Imposition
(Instances when we evaluated as +R and NSs evaluated as –R)

Item 22, Form A: Supposed to be +R; 3 NSs thought –R)

> You are a university student. You are working on a paper
> that is due in two weeks. You need to get a certain book
> for your paper, but it was checked out of the library.
> Your department has a collection of books for the
> students and professors to use. Sometimes students are
> allowed to borrow books from this collection. You lost
> the last book you borrowed. You go to the department
> reading room and talk with the student who is working
> there.
>
> You: _____
> _____
> _____
>
> Student: Okay, but be careful.

APPENDIX C: STRATEGIES USED AND THEIR ABBREVIATIONS

#1 = first occurrence of a strategy
#2 = second occurrence of a strategy

Table C–1: Request Head Act Strategies

STRATEGIES	CODES	DESCRIPTION/EXAMPLE
Preparatory	#1: pr #2: pt	*reference to preparatory condition for feasibility of the request* — Can I borrow...? — Could you move...? — Would you give...?
Strong Hint	#1: st hint #2: sh	*similar to preparatory, but not conventionalized, requires more inferencing* — Will you be going home now? — I wasn't at the lecture.
Want Statement	#1: want #2: wt	*expresses the speakers desire that the request action be carried out* — I'd like to borrow... — I want to see...
Hedged Performative	#1: hp #2: hp	*illocutionary force modified by modals or verbs expressing intention* — I must ask you... — I have to ask you...
Statement of Facts	#1: facts #2: sf	*statement that leaves the hearer no choice* — I have to cancel the meeting.

Table C–2: Request Supportive Move Strategies

STRATEGIES	CODES	DESCRIPTION/EXAMPLE
Grounder	#1: gr #2: gr	*reasons, justifications* — I forgot my notebook.
Disarmer	#1: disarm #2: da	*remove potential objections* — I know you are very busy...?

(continued)

Imposition Minimizer	#1: imp min #2: im	*reduce imposition* — It shouldn't take long.
Preparator	#1: pptr #2: pp	*announcement of request, asking about the availability of something, permission of hearer* — I'd like to ask you something. — Won't you be seeing Mary?
Getting a Pre-Commitment	#1: pre com #2 pc	— Would you do me a favor?
Apology	#1: apol #2: pg	— I'm sorry to bother you.
Gratitude	#1: grat #2: gt	— Thanks for your work last week.

Table C–3: Refusal Head Act Strategies

STRATEGIES	CODES	DESCRIPTION/EXAMPLE
Grounder	#1: gr #2: gr	*excuse, reason, explanation* — I'm going to a party that day.
Statement of Regret	#1: rg #2: rg	— I'm sorry. — I feel terrible.
Non-Performative	#1: np #2: np	— No. — I can't. / don't think so.
Alternative	#1: alt #2: al	— Why don't you ask someone else? — I can have it ready by noon.
Repetition of Original Request	#1: rep req #2 rr	— Help you call people tonight?
Request Help or Empathy	#1: help #2: rh	— I could really use some help.
Wish	#1: wish #2: ws	— I wish I could help. — I'd love / like to help.
Set Condition	#1: set cond #2: sc	— If you had asked me earlier...
Promise of Future Acceptance	#1: fut #2: fa	— Next time I'll do it.

Guilt Trip	#1: guilt #2: gt	— You said you would have it ready by now.
Hedging	#1: hedge #2: hg	— Gee, I don't know. — I'm not sure.

Table C–4: Refusal Supportive Move Strategies

STRATEGIES	CODES	DESCRIPTION/EXAMPLE
Empathy	#1: emp #2: ep	— I realize you are in a difficult situation...
Pause Filler	#1: pause #2: pf	— Uh... — Oh... — Well... — Uhm...
Statement of Positive	#1: pos #2: ps	— That's a good idea.
Gratitude/ Appreciation	#1: grat #2: ga	— Thanks for inviting me.
Imposition Minimizer	#1: imp min #2: im	— We can make the meeting short.

Table C–5: Apology Strategies

STRATEGIES	CODES	DESCRIPTION/EXAMPLE
Sorry	#1: sr #2: sr	— I'm sorry.
Afraid	#1: afr #2: af	— I'm afraid.
Apologize	#1: apol #2: ap	— I apologize.
Forgive	#1: forgv #2: fg	— Forgive me.
Excuse Me	#1: exs #2: xc	— Excuse me.
Explanation	#1: ex #2: ex	"I" *statement with* "I'm sorry" — I'm sorry I missed the bus.

(continued)

Offer of Repair	#1: repair #2: or	*compensation, only if repairable* — I'll buy you a new one.
Lack of Intent	#1: lack #2: li	— I didn't mean to upset you.
Admission of Facts, but Not Responsibility	#1: facts #2: af	*"I" statement without "I'm sorry"* — I missed the bus.
Self Blame	#1: slf blm #2: sb	*self blame*
Expression of Embarrassment	#1: embar #2: ee	*expression of embarrassment*
Statement of Facts, Not Responsibility	#1: nt resp #2: nt	— The bus was late.
Promise of Forbearance	#1: forb #2: pf	*promise it will never happen again* — It will never happen again.
Minimization of Offense	#1: min off #2: mo	— It doesn't look too bad.
Upgrading of Offense	#1: up off #2: uo	— Those papers look important.
Gratitude to Hearer	#1: grat #2: gh	*acknowledgment of hearer's help* — Thanks for waiting.
Distract with Humor	#1: humor #2: dh	— I'm all thumbs!
Distract with Task Oriented Remark	#1: task #2: dt	— Let's look at those pictures.
Statement or Question of Dismay	#1: dismay #2: dm	— What should I do?
Concern for Hearer	#1: concern #2: cn	— Are you all right? — I hope I didn't upset you.

Table C–6: Alerter Strategies

STRATEGIES	CODES	DESCRIPTION/EXAMPLE
Attention Getter	#1: att #2: ag	— Hello. — Excuse me. — Listen.
Surname/Family Name	#1: fam nam #2: sn	— Ms. Lee
First Name	#1: fst nam #2: fn	— Tim
Undetermined Name	#1: und nam #2: un	— [name]
Title/Role	#1: title #2: tr	— Professor — Ma'am

Table C–7: Downgrader Strategies

STRATEGIES	CODES	DESCRIPTION/EXAMPLE
Politeness Markers	#1: polite #2: pm	*bid for cooperation* — Please... — Do you think you could...
Pause Filler	#1: pause #2: pf	— Uh... — Well...
Hedge	#1: hedge #2: hg	*adverbials used to avoid precise* *specification* — Somehow — Kind of
Subjectivizer	#1: subj #2: sj	*expresses speaker's subjective opinion* — I'm afraid — I wonder/think/believe/suppose
Downtoner	#1: dntn #2: dt	*sentential or propositional modifiers* — Perhaps. — Possibly.
Appealer	#1: appeas #2: pl	*elicit a hearer signal, final position* — Will you...? — Okay.

(continued)

Understater	#1: undr #2: us	*adverbial modifiers that under-* *represents the state of affairs* — a bit — a little
Conditional	#1: cd #2: cd	*only if replaceable by an indicative* *form* — I would suggest that...
Conditional Clause	#1: cc #2: cc	— It would fit much better if...
Aspect	#1: asp #2: as	*only if replaceable by a simple form* — I'm wondering if...
Tense	#1: tns #2: tn	*only if past is used with present time* *reference* — I wanted to ask you...

Table C–8: Upgrader Strategies

STRATEGIES	CODES	DESCRIPTION/EXAMPLE
Intensifier	#1: i #2: it	*adverbial modifiers* — very — terribly
Emotional Expressions	#1: emo #2: em	— Oh. — Oh, no. — Oh, God.
Emphasis	#1: emphas #2: ep	*exclamation mark, underlining or* *capitalization, if in written form*
Expletive	#1: expltv #2: xp	— Shit. — Damn.
Lexical Uptoner	#1: lex up #2: lu	— still — as soon as

APPENDIX D: DCT VERSION #1 EXAMPLE PROBLEM ITEMS

Problem Items: Speech Act

Form A #23: This item, which appeared as Form A #6 on DCT version #1, was written in order to elicit an apology. However, when piloted, it elicited requests. So, in the revised version it was, in fact, used as a request item.

Form B #7: This item was also written in order to elicit an apology. However, in the piloting, respondents focused on the realization of their "forgetting" (part of the particular situation), and thus rarely included an apology. The item was rewritten.

Problem Items: Opt Out

Form A #4: This item was designed to elicit a refusal. However, in the piloting, two of the seven NSs opted out. It was decided that the item was too unrealistic and difficult to understand, and thus was rewritten.

Form A #21: For this item instead of refusing, two of the seven NSs carried out the request made of them (loaning a pen). The item was rewritten.

Form A #24: This item as written as a refusal item. However, in the piloting, none of the respondents refused the request made of them (helping a customer). The item was rewritten.

Problem Items: Misinterpretation of P and R Level
Misinterpretation of Power (P)

Form A #7: In order to correct the misinterpretation of power in this item, instead of losing the book of a student officer (first draft), the new item involved losing the computer disk of the head of the department at work.

Form A #12: For this item, the role of the hearer was revised from "secretary" to "manager". Thus the misinterpretation of the degree of power held by the hearer was corrected.

Misinterpretation of Degree of Imposition (R)

<u>Form A #18</u>: Changes to this item involved changing the role of the hearer from a post office worker to a bank teller in order to ensure that the test taker understood that the property damaged in the situation was not public property.

Interestingly enough, the ratings of the speech acts did not always correspond with the actual NS and NNS response. On a few occasions the raters disagreed on the speech act, yet the responses were "correct".

University of Hawai'i at Manoa
National Foreign Language
Resource Center

Form A

Name: _____   Age: _____

Native language: _____   Sex: _____

Years of English study: _____

Directions: Read each of the situations on the following pages. After each situation write what you would say in the situation in a normal conversation.

Example:

Situation: You live in a large apartment building. You are leaving to go to work. On your way out, you meet your next door neighbor, whom you haven't seen for a long time.

You: _____
_____
_____

Situation 1: You live in a large house. You hold the lease to the house and rent out the other rooms. You are in the room of one of your house-mates collecting the rent. You reach to take the rent check when you accidentally knock over a small, empty vase on the desk. It doesn't break.

You: _____
_____
_____

Situation 2: You work in a small shop that repairs jewelry. A valued customer comes into the shop to pick up an antique watch that you know is to be a present. It is not ready yet, even though you promised it would be.

You: _____
_____
_____

Situation 3: You are applying for a new job in a small company and want to make an appointment for an interview. You know the manager is very busy and only schedules interviews in the afternoon from one to four o'clock. However, you currently work in the afternoon. You want to schedule an interview in the morning. You go into the office this morning to turn in your application form when you see the manager.

You: _____
_____
_____

Situation 4: You are a member of the local chapter of a national ski club. Every month the club goes on a ski trip. You are in a club meeting now helping to plan this month's trip. The club president is sitting next to you and asks to borrow a pen. You cannot lend your pen because you only have one and need it to take notes yourself.

You: _____
_____
_____

Situation 5: You work in a small department of a large office. You are in a department meeting now. You need to borrow a pen in order to take some notes. The head of your department is sitting next to you and might have an extra pen.

You: _____
_____
_____

Situation 6: You are an office manager and are interviewing to fill a position that is open. You are interviewing someone now. You walk over to the filing cabinet to get the applicant's application when you accidentally step on a small shopping bag belonging to the applicant. You hear a distinct crunching.

You: _____
_____
_____

Situation 7: You work in a small department of a large office. Last week the head of the department loaned you a computer file on disk. You can't find the disk, and think you have lost it. You have just finished a meeting with your department when the head of the department passes near you.

You: _____
_____
_____

Situation 8: You are shopping for your friend's birthday and see something in a display case. You want to look at it more closely. A salesclerk comes over to you.

You: _____

_____

_____

Situation 9: You live in a large house. You hold the lease to the house and rent out the other rooms. Each person in the house is responsible for a few hours of chores every week. One of your house-mates asks if you can do extra chores this week because they are going out of town. You cannot do your house-mate's chores this week because you are very busy at work this week and do not have any extra time.

You: _____

_____

_____

Situation 10: You are the manager in an office that is now hiring new employees. Last week an applicant came into the office and scheduled an interview for tomorrow. Now, that same person is in the office asking to reschedule the interview because of a family funeral. You cannot reschedule because you are about to leave the country for two weeks, your schedule is completely full, and you need to hire before you leave.

You: _____

_____

_____

Situation 11: You work in a small shop. You are working in the back room when you hear the bell that tells you there is a customer in the front room. You are on the phone making an important business call. You finish the call as quickly as you can and go out to help the waiting customer.

You: _____

_____

_____

Situation 12: You want to apply for a job in a small office. You want to get an application form. You go to the office and see the office manager sitting behind a desk.

You: _____

_____

_____

Situation 13: You are the president of the local chapter of a national hiking club. Every month the club goes on a hiking trip and you are responsible for organizing it. You are on this month's trip and have borrowed another member's hiking book. You are hiking by a river and stop to look at the book. The book slips from your hand, falls in the river and washes away. You hike on to the rest stop where you meet up with the owner of the book.

You: _____
_____
_____

Situation 14: You have worked in a small department of a large office for a number of years and are the head of the department. You have just been given an extra heavy accounting assignment to do. You know that one of your co-workers in the department is especially skilled at bookkeeping. However, you also know that this person is very busy. You want your co-worker to help with the assignment. You go to the desk of your co-worker.

You: _____
_____
_____

Situation 15: You work in a repair shop. One of your valued customers comes in with an antique that is to be a present for a fiftieth wedding anniversary. The customer asks that it be repaired for the party tomorrow. You look at the antique and realize that you cannot do the job in one day. It will take you at least two weeks to finish.

You: _____
_____
_____

Situation 16: You are the president of the local chapter of a national book club. The club reads and discusses a new book every month. You are at this month's meeting, talking with a member of the book club. You need to get the phone number of Sue Lee, another member of the club. You think this person has Sue's number.

You: _____
_____
_____

Situation 17: You are a teacher at a large school. You see the lead teacher on campus. The lead teacher asks you to call all of the other teachers tonight and tell them that there will be a meeting tomorrow. You cannot do it because you know that it will take hours and you have friends coming over to your house tonight.

You: _____
_____
_____

Situation 18: You are in a small bank buying traveler's checks. You move to take the checks when you accidentally knock over a small ceramic figure on the clerk's desk. It doesn't break.

You: _____
_____
_____

Situation 19: You work in a bookstore. You are scheduled to start work at noon today. You will take over for your supervisor who is working the morning shift. You go to work and arrive at the bookstore a few minutes after noon. You see your supervisor.

You: _____
_____
_____

Situation 20: You and a few of your co-workers are working on a special project. You have been appointed the project leader. You had scheduled an afternoon meeting with one of your co-workers, Mary, but she canceled it. You are walking in the hallway when another co-worker also working on the project asks you to give a message to Mary when you see her this afternoon. You cannot deliver the message because you will not be seeing Mary.

You: _____
_____
_____

Situation 21: You are shopping in a department store. You have selected an item and are waiting to pay for it. The salesclerk helps you and explains that there is a special offer on a new product and offers to show you a short demonstration. You cannot watch the demonstration because you are on your way to meet someone for lunch.

You: _____
_____
_____

Situation 22: You rent a room in a large house. The person who holds the lease lives in the house as well. You are responsible for mowing the lawn every week, a job that takes you about two hours to do. You want the lease-holder to mow the lawn for you this week because you are going out of town. You are in the living room when the lease-holder walks in.

You: _____
     _____
     _____

Situation 23: You are an office manager and are hiring to fill a position that has just opened up. Yesterday, many people filled out application forms for the job. The form is very long and takes most people many hours to complete. You are getting ready to interview an applicant, but cannot find the completed application in the files. You want the applicant to resubmit the application. The applicant is now here for the interview.

You: _____
     _____
     _____

Situation 24: You work as a sales clerk in a department store. A customer is paying for an item and should get three dollars back in change. The customer asks that the three dollars be given in quarters, not dollar bills. You cannot give the change because you do not have enough quarters to spare.

You: _____
     _____
     _____

University of Hawai'i at Manoa
National Foreign Language
Resource Center

Form B

Name: _____   Age: _____

Native language: _____   Sex: _____

Years of English study: _____

Directions: Read each of the situations on the following pages. After each situation write what you would say in the situation in a normal conversation.

Example:

Situation: You live in a large apartment building. You are leaving to go to work. On your way out, you meet your next door neighbor, whom you haven't seen for a long time.

You: _____
_____
_____

Situation 1: You work in a small department of a large office. You have worked here for a number of years and are the head of the department. You are in the office of another member of the department in a meeting. You accidentally knock over a framed picture on the desk. It doesn't break.

You: _____
_____
_____

Situation 2: You are applying for a job in a company. You go into the office to turn in your application form to the manager. You talk to the manager for a few minutes. When you move to give the manager your form, you accidentally knock over a vase on the desk and spill water over a pile of papers.

You: _____
_____
_____

Situation 3: You are applying for a student loan at a small bank. You are now meeting with the loan officer. The loan officer is the only person who reviews the applications at this bank. The loan officer tells you that there are many other applicants and that it should take two weeks to review your application. However, you want the loan to be processed as soon as possible in order to pay your tuition by the deadline.

You: _____
_____
_____

Situation 4: You work for a large company. You and a few of your co-workers are working on a special project. You are just finishing a meeting with the group. The leader of the project asks you to give a message to your secretary. You cannot deliver the message because you are going directly to a meeting scheduled at one of the branch offices.

You: _____
_____
_____

Situation 5: You are a member of the local chapter of a national ski club. Every month the club goes on a ski trip. You are in a meeting with the club president, helping plan this month's trip. You want to borrow some paper in order to take some notes.

You: _____
_____
_____

Situation 6: You are shopping in a store that sells handmade crafts. You have shopped here a number of times before and usually make a substantial purchase. Today you are looking for a present for your mother's birthday. You are browsing near a clerk. You pick up a small statuette to get a better look at it and drop it on the floor. It breaks.

You: _____
_____
_____

Situation 7: You rent a room in a large house. The person who holds the lease lives in the house as well. Each person in the house is responsible for a few hours of chores every week. Your chore is to vacuum the house. This morning when you were using the lease-holder's vacuum you accidentally dropped it and now it does not work. You are now in the living room and the lease-holder walks in.

You: _____
_____
_____

Situation 8: You are on an airplane. It is dinner time. The flight attendant sets your food on your tray. You need a napkin.

You: _____
_____
_____

Situation 9: You work in a small department of a large office. You have worked here for a number of years and are the head of the department. You have an important meeting scheduled with another member of your department this afternoon. You are in your office when the member stops in and asks to cancel the meeting in order to work on a special project that is due tomorrow. You cannot schedule the meeting for later because you have to report the information to others at a meeting tomorrow.

You: _____
_____
_____

Situation 10: Last week you had trouble with your company car and took it to a company mechanic. The mechanic promised to have it ready tomorrow morning. You are going on a business trip tomorrow afternoon and need the car. You stop by the repair shop to make sure the repairs will be finished in time. Now the mechanic tells you the shop is very busy and asks if you can wait an extra day for your car. You cannot delay your trip.

You: _____
_____
_____

Situation 11: You are in the airport going through customs after a trip to a foreign country. It is your turn, but when the customs officer asks you for your papers, you realize you do not know where they are. You look in your bag for a little while, find them, and give them to the waiting officer.

You: _____
_____
_____

Situation 12: You work in a restaurant. You have just taken a customer's order and are ready to leave the table. The customer is still holding the menu and you need it for another table.

You: _____
     _____
     _____

Situation 13: You are the president of the local chapter of a national camping club. Every month the club goes on a camping trip and you are responsible for organizing it. Last week you were supposed to meet with another member of the club to plan this month's trip. You had to reschedule because you were too busy. The rescheduled meeting was for 7:30 this morning, but you got caught in heavy traffic and just now arrive at the club headquarters. It is 9:00 a.m.

You: _____
     _____
     _____

Situation 14: You live in a large house. You hold the lease to the house and rent out the other rooms. The washing machine is broken. It is Saturday and the repair person is scheduled to fix it this morning. However, you will not be home because you have to pick up your parents at the airport. You want one of your house-mates to stay home this morning. You are in the kitchen when a house-mate walks in.

You: _____
     _____
     _____

Situation 15: You work in a small printing shop. It is late afternoon and a valued customer comes in to ask if you can print 1500 copies of a new advertisement by tomorrow morning. To do this you would have to work into the night. You are tired after a long day and cannot stay late.

You: _____
     _____
     _____

Situation 16: You work in a small department of a large office. You have worked here for a number of years and are the head of the department. You are in a meeting with the other members of your department. You need to write some notes, but realize you do not have any paper. You turn to the person sitting next to you.

You: _____
     _____
     _____

Situation 17: You are a member of the local chapter of a national camping club. Every month the club goes on a camping trip. The president of the club is responsible for organizing the trips, a job that takes a number of hours. You are on this month's trip talking to the president of the club. The president is going to be out of town for a week and asks you to plan the next trip. You cannot plan the trip because you are going to be very busy with work.

You: _____
_____
_____

Situation 18: You are in a small family-owned restaurant. You go up to the counter to pay your bill. When you reach to hand your check to the restaurant worker you accidentally knock a few of the menus on the floor.

You: _____
_____
_____

Situation 19: You teach in a small school. You have a meeting with the lead teacher for your grade at two o'clock today. When you show up at the meeting it is a few minutes after two.

You: _____
_____
_____

Situation 20: You live in a large house. You hold the lease to the house and rent out the other rooms. You are in the living room when one of your house-mates asks to talk to you. Your house-mate explains that it will only take a few minutes and is not important. However, you cannot talk now because you are on your way out.

You: _____
_____
_____

Situation 21: You are on your lunch hour. You go into a small shop to look for a present. You find something you like and buy it. As you are ready to leave the clerk explains that the store would like to learn more about it's customers and asks if you would fill out a short questionnaire . You cannot fill out the form because you have to hurry back to work.

You: _____
_____
_____

Situation 22: You work for a small department in a large office. The assistant manager of the office gave you a packet of materials to summarize for tomorrow. However, when you start working on the assignment, you realize that you do not have all of the information. You know that the head of the department has the information. You need to get the information, but you know it will take the head of your department about an hour and a half to locate it. You see the head of the department.

You: _____
_____
_____

Situation 23: You are the personnel officer in an office that is now hiring new employees. The application form is quite long and takes most applicants several hours to complete. The form must be typed. An applicant comes in and gives you a completed form. However, it has been typed with a very faint ribbon. The application needs to be retyped.

You: _____
_____
_____

Situation 24: You work in a small store. A customer comes into the store and asks for change for a ten dollar bill. You cannot give the change because you don't have it in the register.

You: _____
_____
_____

University of Hawai'i at Manoa
National Foreign Language
Resource Center

Name: _____   Age: _____

Native language: _____   Sex: _____

Years of English study: _____

Directions: Read each of the situations on the following pages. After each situation write what you would say in the situation in a normal conversation.

Example:

Situation: You live in a large apartment building. You are leaving to go to work. On your way out, you meet your next door neighbor, whom you haven't seen for a long time.

You: _____
_____
_____

Situation 1: You live in a large house. You hold the lease to the house and rent out the other rooms. You and one of your house-mates had planned to meet at 6:00 this evening to talk about something having to do with the house. However, you were late leaving work. It is a few minutes after 6:00 and as you enter the house you see your house-mate waiting in the living room.

You: _____
_____
_____

Situation 2: You are a professional photographer. Last month you took many pictures at a company party. You promised that the prints would be ready for the next company newsletter. The editor of the newsletter comes into your office to pick up the prints, but they are not ready now.

You: _____
_____
_____

Situation 3: You have recently moved to a new city and are looking for an apartment to rent. You are looking at a place now. You like it a lot. The landlord explains that you seem like a good person for the apartment, but that there are a few more people who are interested. The landlord says that you will be called next week and told if you have the place. However, you need the landlord to tell you within the next three days.

You: _____
_____
_____

Situation 4: You are a member of the local chapter of a national hiking club. You are on a hike now. You and a few other hikers have just stopped for a rest. The president of the club sits next to you, takes out a bottle of water to share with everyone. The president offers the bottle to you first. You have brought your own water.

You: _____
_____
_____

Situation 5: You are a member of the local chapter of a national ski club. You are on the club bus and have just arrived at the mountain. You are sitting near the club president. You see that the president is applying sun screen lotion. You want to use the president's lotion because you have forgotten to bring your own. You turn to the club president.

You: _____
_____
_____

Situation 6: You are in a computer store sitting at the desk of a salesperson. You have decided to buy several computers for your business and are handing the payment to the salesperson when you accidentally knock over a cup of coffee on the desk. The coffee spills across the desk and onto the salesperson.

You: _____
_____
_____

Situation 7: You are a member of a local charitable organization. Last week you promised the president of the organization that you would borrow your friend's truck to help move furniture from one office to the another today. However, you found out this morning that you cannot borrow the truck. You are now at the office and see the president.

You: _____
_____
_____

Situation 8: You are shopping in the drug store. You need to buy some envelopes, but cannot find them. You see a salesclerk nearby.

You: _____
_____
_____

Situation 9: You live in a large house. You hold the lease to the house and rent out the other rooms. You are talking with one of your house-mates who mentions that this Saturday is a friend's birthday and that plans have been made to have a party at your house. You cannot allow a party next weekend because you have already scheduled for painters to come and paint the inside of the house that same weekend.

You: _____
_____
_____

Situation 10: You have organized a good-bye party for a co-worker. Everyone in the office has contributed money to have a photograph of all of the office workers framed. The frame store promised that it would be ready today. You go into the store and the clerk tells you that they are very busy now and asks if you can wait another day. You cannot wait because the good-bye party is this evening.

You: _____
_____
_____

Situation 11: You are applying for a loan at a small bank. You have filled out all of the forms and are reaching over the desk to hand them to the loan officer when you accidentally knock over the loan officer's desk calendar.

You: _____
_____
_____

Situation 12: You are a salesperson in a gift shop. You need to get something out of a display case now. However, you are unable to get into the case because a customer is standing in the way and blocking your path.

You: _____
_____
_____

Situation 13: You work in a small department of a large office. You have worked there for a number of years and are the head of the department. Last weekend you borrowed a co-worker's portable computer because you had a lot of extra work to do and were going out of town. However, you accidentally erased some important information that was stored on the computer. It is Monday morning and you see your co-worker.

You: _____
_____
_____

Situation 14: You live in a large house. You hold the lease to the house and rent out the other rooms. Next weekend you are going to put new carpeting in all of the bedrooms. Thus, all of the furniture needs to be moved out of your house-mate's bedroom next weekend. You are sitting in the kitchen when your house-mate enters the room.

You: _____
_____
_____

Situation 15: You are applying for a job in a large company. You have just finished an interview with the manager. The interview went well but took much longer than you expected. You are getting ready to leave the office when the manager explains that it is time for a long tour of the company. You cannot go on the tour because you have another meeting scheduled.

You: _____
_____
_____

Situation 16: You and a few of your co-workers are working on a special project. You have been appointed the project leader. You are working on the project now and are making a few copies on the photocopier. One of your co-workers on the project enters the room. You need a paper clip. You notice that your co-worker has a box of paper clips.

You: _____
_____
_____

Situation 17: You rent a room in a large house. The person who holds the lease lives in the house as well. Each person in the house is responsible for a few hours of chores every week. Your chore is to vacuum the house. The lease holder asks if you can vacuum the house tomorrow afternoon because visitors are coming tomorrow night. You cannot vacuum tomorrow afternoon because you are going to be very busy all day.

You: _____
_____
_____

Situation 18: You are buying four tickets to a movie. You have a coupon for a free ticket. You tell the ticket clerk about the coupon, but when you look for it you can't find it right away. After a little while you find the coupon. You hand it to the clerk.

You: _____
_____
_____

Situation 19: You and a few of your co-workers are working on a special project. You are at a meeting in the office of the project leader. As you are reaching for your briefcase you accidentally knock over the project leader's umbrella which was leaning against the desk.

You: _____
_____
_____

Situation 20: You are the president of the local chapter of a national camping club. You are on a camping trip now. One of the club members is putting on mosquito repellent and offers some to you. You do not need to use the repellent because you have your own.

You: _____
_____
_____

Situation 21: You are a tourist in a large city. You have taken your film to a photo shop. When you go into the shop to pick up the pictures, the salesperson asks if you would like some coupons for more film developing. You do not need the coupons because you are leaving the city today.

You: _____
_____
_____

Situation 22: You work in a small department of a large office. You had an important meeting with the head of your department last week, but you had to cancel it because you got sick. The rescheduled meeting is for this afternoon. You came into the office this morning and felt okay. However, it is now lunch-hour and you are feeling sick again. You want to postpone today's meeting. You go to the office of the department head.

You: _____
_____
_____

Situation 23: Last week you had trouble with your company car. You took it to a company mechanic. You need the car tomorrow for an out of town meeting. You go into the shop to pick it up. Now the mechanic says your car will not be ready until this afternoon. However, you have another meeting this afternoon and do not think that you will get out of the meeting until after the shop closes. You want someone to stay late this afternoon in order for you to pick up your car.

You: _____
_____
_____

Situation 24: You work as a travel agent in a large department store. You are helping a customer at your desk. The customer gets out a packet of bubble-gum, takes a piece, and offers you a piece. You do not like bubble-gum.

You: _____
_____
_____

APPENDIX F: MULTIPLE-CHOICE VERSION #1 ITEM SPECIFICATIONS

The primary source for the linguistic material of the distractors and the correct choice should be actual or modified NNS and NS responses to the situations. The correct choices coming from NS data, the distractors from NNS data. Responses collected should be analyzed to find the major trends in strategy use for NS and NNS. The answer and the distractors should reflect these major trends.

Three main types of differences between the answer and the distractors:

Strategy use:
> For example, for an apology situation the NSs first preference of apology strategy might be the "I'm terribly sorry" strategy, whereas the NNSs might prefer the "Please forgive me" strategy. These differences are mainly pragmalinguistic in nature and stem from transfer.

Sociopragmatic misjudgments:
> These differences stem from a misjudgment of the power, distance, or degree of imposition in the given situation. These differences can manifest themselves through the following:
> — amount of information/degree of specificity
> — degree(s) of politeness, directness and formality — three interrelated concepts.

Phrasing (entirely pragmalinguistic in nature):
> Odd or unusual phrasing due to transfer or ignorance of NS word choices.

In cases where the differences found between NS and NNS data choices seem to be inconsequential or in cases where the NS and NNS choices differ on only one of the elements discussed above, additional differences can be made according the following guidelines.

Considerations

As discussed above there are a number of ways to differentiate the distractors from the correct answer. When choosing distractors from NNS data or when constructing distractors it is suggested that one first consider in this order:

— the type of main move used and its meaning
— the number one supportive strategy used and its meaning

— any other strategies that happen to be key to the cell/situation as determined by the response analysis

Then consider, however, not necessarily in this order:

— the amount of information included, the level of specificity used, and the length of the distractor in comparison to the correct response
— the phrasing used
— the degree of politeness/directness/formality

Take care so that within a move there are no stark differences in meaning that might bias test takers against a choice. For example, in a refusal that includes an alternative as a supportive move, do not have one alternative "I'll do it tomorrow", and another "I'll do it next week". However, there may be cases when stark differences in meaning are employed in order to provide a difference in politeness. This is acceptable.

The three main types of differences are always available in test construction. When using them, keep the considerations outlined above in mind. Use the types of differences resulting from sociopragmatic misjudgments as a guide as you construct or adapt distractors.

University of Hawai'i at Manoa
National Foreign Language
Resource Center

Form A

Name: _____ Age: _____

Native language: _____ Sex: _____

Years of English study: _____

Directions: There are 24 situations on the following pages. Each situation will have three possible responses. Circle the response (a, b, or c) that you think is the most appropriate for the situation described.

Example:

Situation: You live in a large apartment building. You are leaving to go to work. On your way out, you meet your next door neighbor, whom you haven't seen for a long time.

a: Hello. That's a nice shirt. Where did you get it? How much did it cost?

b: Nice to meet you. Tell me where you are going. How is your family?

c: Good morning, Bob. How have you been? We haven't talked for weeks!

Answer: Response "c" is the most appropriate response for this situation. You would circle "c".

a: Hello. That's a nice shirt. Where did you get it? How much did it cost?

b: Nice to meet you. Tell me where you are going. How is your family?

c: Good morning, Bob. How have you been? We haven't talked for weeks!

Situation 1: You live in a large house. You hold the lease to the house and rent out the other rooms. You are in the room of one of your house-mates collecting the rent. You reach to take the rent check when you accidentally knock over a small, empty vase on the desk. It doesn't break.

---

b: Oh! I'm sorry. Thank heavens it didn't break!

c: Oh, I'm sorry. I didn't know there was a vase here.

Situation 2: You work in a small shop that repairs jewelry. A valued customer comes into the shop to pick up an antique watch that you know is to be a present. It is not ready yet, even though you promised it would be.

a: I'm terribly sorry, but your watch is not ready yet. It will take some more time I'm afraid.

b: I'm sorry, but it's not ready yet. Could you come back tomorrow?

c: I'm really sorry, but your watch isn't ready yet. We've been really busy lately. Would it be possible for you to come back tomorrow?

Situation 3: You are applying for a new job in a small company and want to make an appointment for an interview. You know the manager is very busy and only schedules interviews in the afternoon from one to four o'clock. However, you currently work in the afternoon. You want to schedule an interview in the morning. You go into the office this morning to turn in your application form when you see the manager.

a: Excuse me, I'm applying for the recent opening and wanted to get an appointment for an interview. I know that you normally schedule interviews in the afternoon, but I was wondering if you might make an exception for me since I work in the afternoon.

b: I'd like to make an appointment for an interview. I know that you are very busy in the morning, but I have something else to do in the afternoon.

c: Excuse me. I'd like to make a morning appointment for an interview.

Situation 4: You are a member of the local chapter of a national ski club. Every month the club goes on a ski trip. You are in a club meeting now helping to plan this month's trip. The club president is sitting next to you and asks to borrow a pen. You cannot lend your pen because you only have one and need it to take notes yourself.

a: Oh, sorry, it's my only one. Maybe John has an extra, let me check.

b: I'm terribly sorry, this is the only one I have at the moment. Perhaps you might ask John?

c: No, I can't lend this pen. It's my only one.

Form A

Situation 5: You work in a small department of a large office. You are in a department meeting now. You need to borrow a pen in order to take some notes. The head of your department is sitting next to you and might have an extra pen.

a: Excuse me, can I use an extra pen?

b: Oh, I'd like to take some notes, but it seems that I have no pen with me.

c: Excuse me, but do you have an extra pen I could borrow?

Situation 6: You are an office manager and are interviewing to fill a position that is open. You are interviewing someone now. You walk over to the filing cabinet to get the applicant's application when you accidentally step on a small shopping bag belonging to the applicant. You hear a distinct crunching.

a: Oh, I'm sorry.

b: Oh, I'm so sorry! I didn't see your bag — I hope nothing's broken.

c: Oh, I'm sorry. I'm afraid something in this bag broke.

Situation 7: You work in a small department of a large office. Last week the head of the department loaned you a computer file on disk. You can't find the disk, and think you have lost it. You have just finished a meeting with your department when the head of the department passes near you.

a: Say, I can't find the computer disk you loaned me. I think I might have lost it. Do you have a back-up copy?

b: I'm terribly sorry but I have lost the disk I borrowed.

c: Excuse me. Do you remember the disk you let me have the other day? I seem to have misplaced it and am having a hard time finding it. I know you may need it soon, but will you give me another week?

Situation 8: You are shopping for your friend's birthday and see something in a display case. You want to look at it more closely. A salesclerk comes over to you.

a: Excuse me. I want to take a look at that. Will you take it out of the case?

b: Excuse me! Show me that in the case there.

c: Excuse me. May I see that, please?

Situation 9: You live in a large house. You hold the lease to the house and rent out the other rooms. Each person in the house is responsible for a few hours of chores every week. One of your house-mates asks if you can do extra chores this week because they are going out of town. You cannot do your house-mate's chores this week because you are very busy at work this week and do not have any extra time.

a: Oh, I'm sorry. I'm really busy at work this week. Maybe you could ask someone else.

b: No, I can't. I'm very busy this week.

c: I wish I could do it, but I have lots to do... I'm sorry.

Situation 10: You are the manager in an office that is now hiring new employees. Last week an applicant came into the office and scheduled an interview for tomorrow. Now, that same person is in the office asking to reschedule the interview because of a family funeral. You cannot reschedule because you are about to leave the country for two weeks, your schedule is completely full, and you need to hire before you leave.

a: I'm sorry but I cannot find any other time. I'm fully occupied these days, and I'm going abroad soon. Further, I have to have new staff before I leave.

b: I'm very sorry, but my schedule is completely full. I'm about to go to Japan for two weeks and I need to hire someone before I leave.

c: I'm sorry but I can't reschedule the interview because I have an extremely tight schedule.

Situation 11: You work in a small shop. You are working in the back room when you hear the bell that tells you there is a customer in the front room. You are on the phone making an important business call. You finish the call as quickly as you can and go out to help the waiting customer.

a: I'm sorry, I was on the phone, may I help you?

b: I'm so sorry for keeping you waiting. I appreciate your patience.

c: Hello, may I help you? Sorry I was tied up with a phone call. I'm the only one here and I have to do everything, it really is too busy for me alone.

Situation 12: You want to apply for a job in a small office. You want to get an application form. You go to the office and see the office manager sitting behind a desk.

a: Hello. I'm interested in applying for a position with your company. Could I get an application form from you?

b: Excuse me, I would like to apply for a job. So would you give me an application form?

c: Excuse me. I'm thinking of applying for a job here. If it's not too much trouble could I please have an application form?

Situation 13: You are the president of the local chapter of a national hiking club. Every month the club goes on a hiking trip and you are responsible for organizing it. You are on this month's trip and have borrowed another member's hiking book. You are hiking by a river and stop to look at the book. The book slips from your hand, falls in the river and washes away. You hike on to the rest stop where you meet up with the owner of the book.

a: I'm very sorry. I dropped your hiking book into the river and lost it. What should I do?
b: You're not going to believe this! I dropped your book in the river and it washed away. I'm really sorry. I'll replace it immediately when we return home.
c: I'm terribly sorry but I lost your book.

Situation 14: You have worked in a small department of a large office for a number of years and are the head of the department. You have just been given an extra heavy accounting assignment to do. You know that one of your co-workers in the department is especially skilled at bookkeeping. However, you also know that this person is very busy. You want your co-worker to help with the assignment. You go to the desk of your co-worker.

a: I know you are pretty busy, but I just got this extra assignment and it involves bookkeeping. Well, I know you are an expert in bookkeeping.
b: Could you help me out? I've got an assignment that involves bookkeeping.
c: Excuse me, I know you are very busy, but I have this extra assignment I need to do and it involves bookkeeping. Do you think you could help me?

Situation 15: You work in a repair shop. One of your valued customers comes in with an antique that is to be a present for a fiftieth wedding anniversary. The customer asks that it be repaired for the party tomorrow. You look at the antique and realize that you cannot do the job in one day. It will take you at least two weeks to finish.

a: I'm sorry but this can't be completed in just a day. It'll probably take a week or more. Why not give them a card describing the present tomorrow at the party and then give it to them after it's repaired?

b: I'm very sorry to say but it will take about two weeks to repair it. I could have served you if you had brought it in a little earlier.

c: I'm sorry but it will take me at least two weeks to finish.

Situation 16: You are the president of the local chapter of a national book club. The club reads and discusses a new book every month. You are at this month's meeting, talking with a member of the book club. You need to get the phone number of Sue Lee, another member of the club. You think this person has Sue's number.

a: Umm, I need to phone Sue Lee but I don't have her phone number.

b: Excuse me, but I need to get a hold of Sue Lee. Do you have her phone number?

c: Excuse me, but do you happen to have Sue Lee's phone number by any chance? I need to call her but I don't have the number with me.

Situation 17: You are a teacher at a large school. You see the lead teacher on campus. The lead teacher asks you to call all of the other teachers tonight and tell them that there will be a meeting tomorrow. You cannot do it because you know that it will take hours and you have friends coming over to your house tonight.

a: Oh, I have a very tight schedule tonight. Could you ask somebody else?

b: I'm terribly sorry but I can't. My evening is all tied up tonight because my friends are coming over for dinner. Maybe another teacher could help. Really, I'm sorry! I'll help next time.

c: I'm sorry, but I have friends coming over to my house tonight, so I won't have time. Maybe you could ask one of the other teachers.

Situation 18: You are in a small bank buying traveler's checks. You move to take the checks when you accidentally knock over a small ceramic figure on the clerk's desk. It doesn't break.

a: Oh, I'm sorry. Hope it doesn't have any damage.

b: Oops! I'm sorry. Is there anything wrong with that?

c: Oh, I'm sorry! I'm glad it didn't break.

Situation 19: You work in a bookstore. You are scheduled to start work at noon today. You will take over for your

supervisor who is working the morning shift. You go to work and
arrive at the bookstore a few minutes after noon. You see your
supervisor.

a: I am sorry to be late. I am sure this is the last time I'll
   be late.
b: Sorry I'm a little late — the traffic was awful!
c: Sorry I am late.

Situation 20: You and a few of your co-workers are working on a
special project. You have been appointed the project leader.
You had scheduled an afternoon meeting with one of your co-
workers, Many, but she canceled it. You are walking in the
hallway when another co-worker also working on the project asks
you to give a message to Mary when you see her this afternoon.
You cannot deliver the message because you will not be seeing
Mary.

a: Sorry. The meeting has been canceled, so I won't be seeing
   Mary this afternoon.
b: Sorry, but I can't. I won't be seeing her because the
   meeting was canceled today.
c: I'm sorry but I don't think I can give a message to Mary
   since she canceled the meeting earlier today. I hope the
   message isn't too important!

Situation 21: You are shopping in a department store. You have
selected an item and are waiting to pay for it. The salesclerk
helps you, explains that there is a special offer on a new
product, and offers to show you a short demonstration. You
cannot watch the demonstration because you are on your way to
meet someone for lunch.

a: No, I can't. I'm in a hurry.
b: Excuse me, but I've got to go. I'm already late for meeting
   someone, you know.
c: I'm sorry, but I've got a lunch date.

Situation 22: You rent a room in a large house. The person who
holds the lease lives in the house as well. You are responsible
for mowing the lawn every week, a job that takes you about two
hours to do. You want the lease-holder to mow the lawn for you
this week because you are going out of town. You are in the
living room when the lease-holder walks in.

a: Excuse me, I have a favor to ask you. I have to go out of
   town this week, so would you please mow the lawn for me?

b: Say, I'm going out of town this week, so I won't be able to mow the lawn. Would you mind doing it while I'm away or should we just leave it until I get back?

c: Excuse me, I'm going out of town next week, so would you mow the lawn for me then?

Situation 23: You are an office manager and are hiring to fill a position that has just opened up. Yesterday, many people filled out application forms for the job. The form is very long and takes most people many hours to complete. You are getting ready to interview an applicant, but cannot find the completed application in the files. You want the applicant to resubmit the application. The applicant is now here for the interview.

a: I'm sorry but I would like you to completely fill out the application form.

b: I'm very sorry, but we seem to have misplaced your application. After the interview would you mind filling out another one?

c: I'm sorry I cannot find your application form. You'll have to fill it out again.

Situation 24: You work as a sales clerk in a department store. A customer is paying for an item and should get three dollars back in change. The customer asks that the three dollars be given in quarters, not dollar bills. You cannot give the change because you do not have enough quarters to spare.

a: I'm sorry but I don't have enough quarters.

b: No, I can't give you the quarters because I don't have enough.

c: I'm sorry, I don't have enough quarters. I could give you two singles and four quarters.

University of Hawai'i at Manoa
National Foreign Language
Resource Center

Name: _____   Age: _____

Native language: _____   Sex: _____

Years of English study: _____

Directions: There are 24 situations on the following pages. Each situation will have three possible responses. Circle the response (a, b, or c) that you think is the most appropriate for the situation described.

Example:

Situation: You live in a large apartment building. You are leaving to go to work. On your way out, you meet your next door neighbor, whom you haven't seen for a long time.

a: Hello. That's a nice shirt. Where did you get it? How much did it cost?

b: Nice to meet you. Tell me where you are going. How is your family?

c: Good morning, Bob. How have you been? We haven't talked for weeks!

Answer: Response "c" is the most appropriate response for this situation. You would circle "c".

a: Hello. That's a nice shirt. Where did you get it? How much did it cost?

b: Nice to meet you. Tell me where you are going. How is your family?

c: Good morning, Bob. How have you been? We haven't talked for weeks!

Situation 1: You work in a small department of a large office. You have worked here for a number of years and are the head of the department. You are in the office of another member of the department in a meeting. You accidentally knock over a framed picture on the desk. It doesn't break.

a: Oh!

b: Oh! Sorry.

c: Oh, this picture frame is stiff. It hurt me!

Situation 2: You are applying for a job in a company. You go into the office to turn in your application form to the manager. You talk to the manager for a few minutes. When you move to give the manager your form, you accidentally knock over a vase on the desk and spill water over a pile of papers.

a: Oh, I'm very sorry. How terrible! All your papers are wet now.

b: Oh, I'm sorry.

c: Oh, I'm so sorry! Where can I get some paper towels to clean this up?

Situation 3: You are applying for a student loan at a small bank. You are now meeting with the loan officer. The loan officer is the only person who reviews the applications at this bank. The loan officer tells you that there are many other applicants and that it should take two weeks to review your application. However, you want the loan to be processed as soon as possible in order to pay your tuition by the deadline.

a: I'm sorry I am applying so late, but the tuition payment deadline is on the tenth of the month. Could you possibly try to get the processing speeded up so I could pay my tuition on time?

b: Seems like lot of people want to get student loans. You must be really busy. I'm very happy that I have an opportunity to apply. However, I have to pay my tuition as soon as possible, I wonder if there is any way I could do this...

c: Could you review my application as soon as possible? The deadline to pay my tuition is very near.

Situation 4: You work for a large company. You and a few of your co-workers are working on a special project. You are just finishing a meeting with the group. The leader of the project asks you to give a message to your secretary. You cannot deliver the message because you are going directly to a meeting scheduled at one of the branch offices.

a: I'm sorry, but I'm going straight to another meeting. I won't be going back to my office until 4 o'clock.

b: I wish I could complete your mission right away but I have to go to another meeting directly from here. If it's all right to deliver it after my other meeting I'm happy to do so.

c: Would you mind asking someone else? I've got to go to another meeting right now.

Situation 5: You are a member of the local chapter of a national ski club. Every month the club goes on a ski trip. You are in a meeting with the club president, helping plan this month's trip. You want to borrow some paper in order to take some notes.

a: Excuse me, please give me some paper.

b: Oh, I'd like to take some notes, but it seems that I have no paper with me.

c: Could I borrow some paper?

Situation 6: You are shopping in a store that sells handmade crafts. You have shopped here a number of times before and usually make a substantial purchase. Today you are looking for a present for your mother's birthday. You are browsing near a clerk. You pick up a small statuette to get a better look at it and accidentally drop it on the floor. It breaks.

a: Oh, I'm sorry.

b: Oh, I'm so sorry. Can I pay for it?

c: Oh. I'm sorry. But I'm covered under an insurance. I'm glad of that.

Situation 7: You rent a room in a large house. The person who holds the lease lives in the house as well. Each person in the house is responsible for a few hours of chores every week. Your chore is to vacuum the house. This morning when you were using the lease-holder's vacuum you accidentally dropped it and now it does not work. You are now in the living room and the lease-holder walks in.

a: I'm sorry, but I accidentally broke your vacuum cleaner. I was using it this morning and I dropped it and now it doesn't work. Do you know where I can get it repaired?

b: I just wrecked your vacuum cleaner. What should I do?

c: It's strange the vacuum cleaner suddenly stopped working, after I dropped it just now. But I don't think it was so hard.

Situation 8: You are on an airplane. It is dinner time. The flight attendant sets your food on your tray. You need a napkin.

a: Excuse me, I seem to be missing a napkin. Could you give me one?

b: Excuse me! Give me a napkin.

c: Excuse me, could I have a napkin please?

Situation 9: You work in a small department of a large office. You have worked here for a number of years and are the head of the department. You have an important meeting scheduled with another member of your department this afternoon. You are in your office when the member stops in and asks to cancel the meeting in order to work on a special project that is due tomorrow. You cannot schedule the meeting for later because you have to report the information to others at a meeting tomorrow.

a: I'm sorry but we can't postpone this meeting. It is very important since I have to report on the information at a meeting tomorrow. I'll try to make it short.

b: No, I can't. I need that information today.

c: I wish I could do it, but I have to report on the meeting tomorrow, so...

Situation 10: Last week you had trouble with your company car and took it to a company mechanic. The mechanic promised to have it ready tomorrow morning. You are going on a business trip tomorrow afternoon and need the car. You stop by the repair shop to make sure the repairs will be finished in time. Now the mechanic tells you the shop is very busy and asks if you can wait an extra day for your car. You cannot delay your trip.

a: But you promised to fix it by tomorrow morning. Look, I'm going on a business trip and I do need the car. Please hurry.

b: Sorry, I can't. I really need the car tomorrow morning because I'm going on a trip.

c: No, I can't wait a day. I have to go on a trip tomorrow, and I need the car. You said you'd repair the car by tomorrow.

Situation 11: You are in the airport going through customs after a trip to a foreign country. It is your turn, but when the customs officer asks you for your papers, you realize you do not know where they are. You look in your bag for a little while, find them, and give them to the waiting officer.

a: Oh, here they are. I knew they were in here somewhere. Sorry it took so long.

b: Oh I found them! Thank you for your patience. I'll keep
them together with me next time.

c: Sorry.

Situation 12: You work in a restaurant. You have just taken a
customer's order and are ready to leave the table. The customer
is still holding the menu and you need it.

a: Excuse me, are you finished with that?

b: Excuse me, would you give me that menu? I need it

c: Excuse me. If it's not too much trouble could I please take
your menu?

Situation 13: You are the president of the local chapter of a
national camping club. Every month the club goes on a camping
trip and you are responsible for organizing it. Last week you
were supposed to meet with another member of the club to plan
this month's trip. You had to reschedule because you were too
busy. The rescheduled meeting was for 7:30 this morning, but
you got caught in heavy traffic and just now arrive at the club
headquarters. It is 9:00 a.m.

a: I'm terribly sorry. I got caught in a traffic jam. It was
terrible. Anyway, I rescheduled the meeting and came late.
I'm sorry.

b: I'm really sorry I'm so late. I got caught in a terrible
traffic jam. Do you still want to meet or is it too late
now?

c: I'm terribly sorry to be late. But I couldn't help it. I
got caught in a traffic jam.

Situation 14: You live in a large house. You hold the lease to
the house and rent out the other rooms. The washing machine is
broken. It is Saturday and the repair person is scheduled to
fix it this morning. However, you will not be home because you
have to pick up your parents at the airport. You want one of
your house-mates to stay home this morning. You are in the
kitchen when a house-mate walks in.

a: Hi, how are you today? I have to go to the airport to pick
up my parents but a repair person is coming while I'm gone
to the airport. He's coming to fix the washing machine.

b: Would you mind staying home this morning? I've got to go to
the airport to pick up my parents.

c: Are you going to be around this morning? I need someone to
be here when the washing machine repair person comes. I
have to go to the airport to pick up my parents.

Situation 15: You work in a small printing shop. It is late afternoon and a valued customer comes in to ask if you can print 1500 copies of a new advertisement by tomorrow morning. To do this you would have to work into the night. You are tired after a long day and cannot stay late.

a: I'm sorry but we're closing soon. I really can't do it by tomorrow morning, but if you can come back I can finish it by tomorrow afternoon.

b: I'm sorry but I can't help you. In order to help you I would have to work into the night, but I have to go home and feed my kids. Sorry about that.

c: Well, I hate to tell you, but it would be impossible to prepare 1500 copies by tomorrow morning.

Situation 16: You work in a small department of a large office. You have worked here for a number of years and are the head of the department. You are in a meeting with the other members of your department. You need to write some notes, but realize you do not have any paper. You turn to the person sitting next to you.

a: Excuse me, I'd like to take some notes, but I forgot to bring any paper.

b: Could I please borrow some paper?

c: Excuse me, might I borrow some paper? I seem not to have any with me.

Situation 17: You are a member of the local chapter of a national camping club. Every month the club goes on a camping trip. The president of the club is responsible for organizing the trips, a job that takes a number of hours. You are on this month's trip talking to the president of the club. The president is going to be out of town for a week and asks you to plan the next trip. You cannot plan the trip because you are going to be very busy with work.

a: I can't. I'm going to be very busy. Can't you ask somebody else?

b: Oh, I wish I could do it, but the thing is, I'm now really busy with my work, and I'm afraid I have no time to do anything else. I'm sorry.

c: I'd like to help out, but I can't this week. I've got a really busy schedule at work this week.

Situation 18: You are in a small family-owned restaurant. You go up to the counter to pay your bill. When you reach to hand your check to the restaurant worker, you accidentally knock a few of the menus on the floor.

a: Oh, I'm sorry. I hope I didn't make them dirty.
b: Oh, I hope I didn't get them dirty. Let me pick them up for you, please.
c: Oops! Sorry. Let me get them.

Situation 19: You teach in a small school. You have a meeting with the lead teacher for your grade at two o'clock today. When you show up at the meeting it is a few minutes after two.

a: Sorry to be late. But it is no big deal.
b: Sorry I'm late.
c: Hi!

Situation 20: You live in a large house. You hold the lease to the house and rent out the other rooms. You are in the living room when one of your house-mates asks to talk to you. Your house-mate explains that it will only take a few minutes and is not important. However, you cannot talk now because you are on your way out.

a: Sorry. Can it wait until later? I've got to leave now or I'll be late.
b: I can't talk to you now. Let's talk later.
c: I'm sorry, but I'm on my way out right now and I'd rather not be late. Postpone it until I come back, please?

Situation 21: You are on your lunch hour. You go into a small shop to look for a present for your friend's birthday. You find something you like and buy it. As you are ready to leave the clerk explains that the would like to learn more about it's customers and asks if you would fill out a short questionnaire. You cannot fill out the form because you have to hurry back to work.

a: No, I must go back to work right now. Will you ask somebody else?
b: I wish I could but I'll be late for my work so I can't. Sorry.
c: Sorry, but I'm in a hurry.

Situation 22: You work for a small department in a large office. The assistant manager of the office gave you a packet of materials to summarize for tomorrow. However, when you start working on the assignment, you realize that you do not have all of the information. You know that the head of the department has the information. You need to get the information, but you know it will take the head of your department about an hour and a half to locate it. You see the head of the department.

a: Could you do me a favor? I hate to ask you but I need the information on last year's financial report. Could you find that for me?

b: I'm working on this summary for tomorrow but the materials Mary gave me aren't complete. I really need last year's financial report. Could I get that from you?

c: Hi. The assistant manager told me to summarize these materials by tomorrow but I need last year's financial report from you in order to continue. Can you give it to me, please?

Situation 23: You are the personnel officer in an office that is now hiring new employees. The application form is quite long and takes most applicants several hours to complete. The form must be typed. An applicant comes in and gives you a completed form. However, it has been typed with a very faint ribbon. The application needs to be retyped.

a: Well, it looks fine but it's hard to read the letters. May I ask you to type it again to have them clearer?

b: I'm sorry, but you'll have to retype this in order for anyone to be able to read it.

c: I regret to say this application needs to be retyped. This is illegible because it was typed with a very faint ribbon.

Situation 24: You work in a small store. A customer comes into the store and asks for change for a ten dollar bill. You cannot give the change because you don't have it in the register.

a: I'm sorry, we don't have change for a ten dollar bill.

b: No, we are short of change, sorry.

c: I'm sorry, but I don't have change for a ten right now. Maybe you could try next door.

University of Hawai'i at Manoa
National Foreign Language
Resource Center

Form C

Name: _____   Age: _____

Native language: _____   Sex: _____

Years of English study: _____

Directions: There are 24 situations on the following pages. Each situation will have three possible responses. Circle the response (a, b, or c) that you think is the most appropriate for the situation described.

Example:

Situation: You live in a large apartment building. You are leaving to go to work. On your way out, you meet your next door neighbor, whom you haven't seen for a long time.

a: Hello. That's a nice shirt. Where did you get it? How much did it cost?

b: Nice to meet you. Tell me where you are going. How is your family?

c: Good morning, Bob. How have you been? We haven't talked for weeks!

Answer: Response "c" is the most appropriate response for this situation. You would circle "c".

a: Hello. That's a nice shirt. Where did you get it? How much did it cost?

b: Nice to meet you. Tell me where you are going. How is your family?

c: Good morning, Bob. How have you been? We haven't talked for weeks!

Situation 1: You live in a large house. You hold the lease to the house and rent out the other rooms. You and one of your house-mates had planned to meet at 6:00 this evening to talk about something having to do with the house. However, you were late leaving work. It is a few minutes after 6:00 and as you enter the house you see your house-mate waiting in the living room.

a: Hi!

b: Hi. Sorry I'm late. I didn't get out of the office until late.

c: I am sorry to be late. I had a lot of things to do this afternoon.

Situation 2: You are a professional photographer. Last month you took many pictures at a company party. You promised that the prints would be ready for the next company newsletter. The editor of the newsletter comes into your office to pick up the prints, but they are not ready now.

a: Hello. I'm sorry but the pictures are not ready yet. Could you call me up before you come here? I'm sure I'll get them done by this afternoon.

b: I'm sorry they are not ready.

c: Oh, I'm very sorry, but the prints are not ready right now. I'll have them ready by this afternoon.

Situation 3: You have recently moved to a new city and are looking for an apartment to rent. You are looking at a place now. You like it a lot. The landlord explains that you seem like a good person for the apartment, but that there are a few more people who are interested. The landlord says that you will be called next week and told if you have the place. However, you need the landlord to tell you within the next three days.

a: I'd really like this apartment, but I can't wait until next week. Is there any way you could let me know in the next 3 days?

b: Oh, well, I really like this apartment, but I have to know a little sooner than that, if that's possible...

c: Could it be possible to find out a little earlier? I need to know that this week.

Situation 4: You are a member of the local chapter of a national hiking club. You are on a hike now. You and a few other hikers have just stopped for a rest. The president of the club sits next to you, takes out a bottle of water to share with everyone. The president offers the bottle to you first. You have brought your own water.

a: Thanks, but I've got my own.

b: Oh, no thank you. I've got my own bottle. I'll pass this on to the next person.

c: No, thank you.

Situation 5: You are a member of the local chapter of a national ski club. You are on the club bus and have just arrived at the mountain. You are sitting near the club president. You see that the president is applying sun screen lotion. You want to use the president's lotion because you have forgotten to bring your own. You turn to the club president.

a: May I have your lotion?

b: Oh no. I forgot my sun screen.

c: Could I use a little of your sun screen? I forgot to pack mine.

Situation 6: You are in a computer store sitting at the desk of a salesperson. You have decided to buy several computers for your business and are handing the payment to the salesperson when you accidentally knock over a cup of coffee on the desk. The coffee spills across the desk and onto the salesperson.

a: Oh, I'm sorry.

b: Oh! I'm so sorry! Let me help clean it up.

c: Oh, what should I do?! Are you all right? I am terribly sorry.

Situation 7: You are a member of a local charitable organization. Last week you promised the president of the organization that you would borrow your friend's truck to help move furniture from one office to the another today. However, you found out this morning that you cannot borrow the truck. You are now at the office and see the president.

a: I'm really sorry. I've just found out I can't borrow my friend's truck today. Do we know anyone else who might be able to lend us a truck?

b: I'm so sorry. I couldn't borrow the truck.

c: I am very sorry, but this morning I found out that I cannot borrow the truck. What should we do? I am really sorry that I couldn't keep my promise.

Situation 8: You are shopping in the drug store. You need to buy some envelopes, but cannot find them. You see a salesclerk nearby.

a: Excuse me. I need to buy some envelopes to send some letters. Where can I find them?

b: Excuse me! Show me the envelopes.

c: Excuse me, where are the envelopes?

Situation 9: You live in a large house. You hold the lease to
the house and rent out the other rooms. You are talking with
one of your house-mates who mentions that this Saturday is a
friend's birthday and that plans have been made to have a party
at your house. You cannot allow a party next weekend because
you have already scheduled for painters to come and paint the
inside of the house that same weekend.

a: I'm sorry, but it won't work out for next weekend. The
   house is being painted then. You'll have to do it another
   time.
b: You can't have a party next weekend. The painters are
   coming that weekend.
c: Oh, why didn't you tell me the plan earlier? I'm having the
   rooms painted next weekend. How many people are coming? Can
   you postpone it to the weekend after? The house will look
   nicer for the party. Or shall I change my schedule?

Situation 10: You have organized a good-bye party for a co-
worker. Everyone in the office has contributed money to have a
photograph of all of the office workers framed. The frame store
promised that it would be ready today. You go into the store
and the clerk tells you that they are very busy now and asks if
you can wait another day. You cannot wait because the good-bye
party is this evening.

a: Oh! I'll be in trouble; I don't know if we can wait for
   tomorrow. I'm supposed to pick it up today. I'll talk to my
   manager and see if we can wait a couple more hours.
b: No, I can't wait. It's a gift for a good-bye party tonight,
   so I need it done by 5 o'clock today.
c: I can't wait. I need it this evening. You promised it would
   be ready today, didn't you?

Situation 11: You are applying for a loan at a small bank. You
have filled out all of the forms and are reaching over the desk
to hand them to the loan officer when you accidentally knock
over the loan officer's desk calendar.

a: Oops, sorry about that.
b: Oh my. I'm quite sorry. I do hope it isn't harmed.
c: Oh, I'm sorry. I didn't break anything.

Situation 12: You are a salesperson in a gift shop. You need to
get something out of a display case now. However, you are
unable to get into the case because a customer is standing in
the way and blocking your path.

a: Excuse me. I need to get to the case behind you.

b: Excuse me. Could you clear the way? I have to get things out of the display case.

c: Excuse me. If it's not too much trouble, might I get into that display case?

Situation 13: You work in a small department of a large office. You have worked there for a number of years and are the head of the department. Last weekend you borrowed a co-worker's portable computer because you had a lot of extra work to do and were going out of town. However, you accidentally erased some important information that was stored on the computer. It is Monday morning and you see your co-worker.

a: Hi, I'm terribly sorry, but I accidentally erased information stored on your computer. I really apologize to you for my carelessness. Do you have a backup copy of that?

b: Hi, I've got some bad news for you. I accidentally erased some stuff on your hard drive. I'm really sorry. Did you have a back-up copy?

c: I'm terribly sorry. I erased some information on the computer.

Situation 14: You live in a large house. You hold the lease to the house and rent out the other rooms. Next weekend you are going to put new carpeting in all of the bedrooms. Thus, all of the furniture needs to be moved out of your house-mate's bedroom next weekend. You are sitting in the kitchen when your house-mate enters the room.

a: Hi. Do you think you will be around next weekend? I'm planning to put new carpeting in the bedrooms next weekend.

b: Would you mind helping out next weekend? I'm going to put in new carpet.

c: Hi, we're going to be getting new carpet next weekend, so do you think you could move the furniture out of your room next Saturday?

Situation 15: You are applying for a job in a large company. You have just finished an interview with the manager. The interview went well but took much longer than you expected. You are getting ready to leave the office when the manager explains that it is time for a long tour of the company. You cannot go on the tour because you have another meeting scheduled.

a: I'm sorry, I didn't realize there would be a tour. I've scheduled a meeting that starts in twenty minutes. Would it be possible to do the tour another time?

b: Oh, I didn't know about the tour and I have an appointment in twenty minutes.

c: I am very sorry, but I cannot go on the tour. I was not informed, and besides, I have another appointment this afternoon.

Situation 16: You and a few of your co-workers are working on a special project. You have been appointed the project leader. You are working on the project now and are making a few copies on the photocopier. One of your co-workers on the project enters the room. You need a paper clip. You notice that your co-worker has a box of paper clips.

a: Oh, it seems I need a paper clip.

b: Hi. Could I borrow a paper clip?

c: Might I borrow a paper clip? I seem not to have any with me.

Situation 17: You rent a room in a large house. The person who holds the lease lives in the house as well. Each person in the house is responsible for a few hours of chores every week. Your chore is to vacuum the house. The lease holder asks if you can vacuum the house tomorrow afternoon because visitors are coming tomorrow night. You cannot vacuum tomorrow afternoon because you are going to be very busy all day.

a: Oh, I can't do it tomorrow afternoon, I'm going to be busy all day.

b: No, I cannot vacuum the house tomorrow because I am very busy with exams. I am sorry but could you do it yourself?

c: I'm sorry but I'm busy all day tomorrow. How about if I do as much as I can tonight?

Situation 18: You are buying four tickets to a movie. You have a coupon for a free ticket. You tell the ticket clerk about the coupon, but when you look for it you can't find it right away. After a little while you find the coupon. You hand it to the clerk.

a: Oh, here it is. This is a coupon for a free ticket.

b: Oh, my. I am so sorry I'm so slow.

c: Here it is. Sorry it took so long.

Situation 19: You and a few of your co-workers are working on a special project. You are at a meeting in the office of the project leader. As you are reaching for your briefcase you accidentally knock over the project leader's umbrella which was leaning against the desk.

a: Oh, I am sorry. I didn't notice that it was there. Is it new?
b: Oh, sorry about that.
c: Oh.

Situation 20: You are the president of the local chapter of a national camping club. You are on a camping trip now. One of the club members is putting on mosquito repellent and offers some to you. You do not need to use the repellent because you have your own.

a: No thanks. I've got my own.
b: I don't need it.
c: Oh, no thank you. I've got some really good mosquito repellent of my own. I think I'll use that.

Situation 21: You are a tourist in a large city. You have taken your film to a photo shop. When you go into the shop to pick up the pictures, the salesperson asks if you would like some coupons for more film developing. You do not need the coupons because you are leaving the city today.

a: No. I really don't want any.
b: Thanks but I don't need them because I'm going to leave this city soon.
c: No thanks, I'm leaving town today.

Situation 22: You work in a small department of a large office. You had an important meeting with the head of your department last week, but you had to cancel it because you got sick. The rescheduled meeting is for this afternoon. You came into the office this morning and felt okay. However, it is now lunch-hour and you are feeling sick again. You want to postpone today's meeting. You go to the office of the department head.

a: Um, about today's meeting. Do you think I can postpone it again? I felt OK this morning but I'm feeling sick again now.
b: I'm sorry, but I'm still not feeling very well. Could we reschedule the meeting again?
c: I'm sorry, but I'm still sick. Let's reschedule the meeting.

Situation 23: Last week you had trouble with your company car. You took it to a company mechanic. You need the car tomorrow for an out of town meeting. You go into the shop to pick it up. Now the mechanic says your car will not be ready until this afternoon. However, you have another meeting this afternoon and do not think that you will get out of the meeting until after the shop closes. You want someone to stay late this afternoon in order for you to pick up your car.

a: I was told that my car would be ready this afternoon, but I guess I cannot pick it up before this shop closes because of a long meeting scheduled for this afternoon. I want someone to stay late this afternoon so that I can pick it up, but is this possible?

b: I really need my car today, but I won't be able to come in before closing time. Would it be possible for someone to stay a little late so I can pick it up?

c: Well, I can't pick up the car this afternoon until very late. I have an important meeting that I have to stay in all afternoon. I need the car first thing in the morning tomorrow. I need to ask someone to stay late in order for me to pick up my car after my meeting.

Situation 24: You work as a travel agent in a large department store. You are helping a customer at your desk. The customer gets out a packet of bubble-gum, takes a piece, and offers you a piece. You do not like bubble-gum.

a: Thank you, but I'm not allowed to have anything while on duty.

b: No. I don't want any.

c: No, thank you

University of Hawai'i at Manoa
National Foreign Language
Resource Center

Form A

Name: _____   Age: _____

Native language: _____   Sex: _____

Years of English study: _____

Directions: You will hear descriptions of 24 different situations. Each situation will be repeated once. After the repetition, say what you would say if you were in the situation described.

Example:

Situation: You live in a large apartment building. You are leaving to go to work. On your way out, you meet your next door neighbor, whom you haven't seen for a long time.

[repetition of situation]

You say:

Situation 1: You live in a large house. You hold the lease to the house and rent out the other rooms. You are in the room of one of your house-mates collecting the rent. You reach to take the rent check when you accidentally knock over a small, empty vase on the desk. It doesn't break.

You say:

Situation 2: You work in a small shop that repairs jewelry. A valued customer comes into the shop to pick up an antique watch that you know is to be a present. It is not ready yet, even though you promised it would be.

You say:

Situation 3: You are applying for a new job in a small company and want to make an appointment for an interview. You know the manager is very busy and only schedules interviews in the afternoon from one to four o'clock. However, you currently work in the afternoon. You want to schedule an interview in the morning. You go into the office this morning to turn in your application form when you see the manager.

You say:

Situation 4: You are a member of the local chapter of a national ski club. Every month the club goes on a ski trip. You are in a club meeting now helping to plan this month's trip. The club president is sitting next to you and asks to borrow a pen. You cannot lend your pen because you only have one and need it to take notes yourself.

You say:

Situation 5: You work in a small department of a large office. You are in a department meeting now. You need to borrow a pen in order to take some notes. The head of your department is sitting next to you and might have an extra pen.

You say:

Situation 6: You are an office manager and are interviewing to fill a position that is open. You are interviewing someone now. You walk over to the filing cabinet to get the applicant's application when you accidentally step on a small shopping bag belonging to the applicant. You hear a distinct crunching.

You say:

Situation 7: You work in a small department of a large office. Last week the head of the department loaned you a computer file on disk. You can't find the disk, and think you have lost it. You have just finished a meeting with your department when the head of the department passes near you.

You say:

Situation 8: You are shopping for your friend's birthday and see something in a display case. You want to look at it more closely. A salesclerk comes over to you.

You say:

Situation 9: You live in a large house. You hold the lease to the house and rent out the other rooms. Each person in the house is responsible for a few hours of chores every week. One of your house-mates asks if you can do extra chores this week because they are going out of town. You cannot do your house-mate's chores this week because you are very busy at work this week and do not have any extra time.

You say:

Situation 10: You are the manager in an office that is now hiring new employees. Last week an applicant came into the office and scheduled an interview for tomorrow. Now, that same person is in the office asking to reschedule the interview because of a family funeral. You cannot reschedule because you are about to leave the country for two weeks, your schedule is completely full, and you need to hire before you leave.

You say:

Situation 11: You work in a small shop. You are working in the back room when you hear the bell that tells you there is a customer in the front room. You are on the phone making an important business call. You finish the call as quickly as you can and go out to help the waiting customer.

You say:

Situation 12: You want to apply for a job in a small office. You want to get an application form. You go to the office and see the office manager sitting behind a desk.

You say:

Situation 13: You are the president of the local chapter of a national hiking club. Every month the club goes on a hiking trip and you are responsible for organizing it. You are on this month's trip and have borrowed another member's hiking book. You are hiking by a river and stop to look at the book. The book slips from your hand, falls in the river and washes away. You hike on to the rest stop where you meet up with the owner of the book.

You say:

Situation 14: You have worked in a small department of a large office for a number of years and are the head of the department. You have just been given an extra heavy accounting assignment to do. You know that one of your co-workers in the department is especially skilled at bookkeeping. However, you also know that this person is very busy. You want your co-worker to help with the assignment. You go to the desk of your co-worker.

You say:

Situation 15: You work in a repair shop. One of your valued customers comes in with an antique that is to be a present for a fiftieth wedding anniversary. The customer asks that it be repaired for the party tomorrow. You look at the antique and realize that you cannot do the job in one day. It will take you at least two weeks to finish.

You say:

Situation 16: You are the president of the local chapter of a national book club. The club reads and discusses a new book every month. You are at this month's meeting, talking with a member of the book club. You need to get the phone number of Sue Lee, another member of the club. You think this person has Sue's number.

You say:

Situation 17: You are a teacher at a large school. You see the lead teacher on campus. The lead teacher asks you to call all of the other teachers tonight and tell them that there will be a meeting tomorrow. You cannot do it because you know that it will take hours and you have friends coming over to your house tonight.

You say:

Situation 18: You are in a small bank buying traveler's checks. You move to take the checks when you accidentally knock over a small ceramic figure on the clerk's desk. It doesn't break.

You say:

Situation 19: You work in a bookstore. You are scheduled to start work at noon today. You will take over for your supervisor who is working the morning shift. You go to work and arrive at the bookstore a few minutes after noon. You see your supervisor.

You say:

Situation 20: You and a few of your co-workers are working on a special project. You have been appointed the project leader. You had scheduled an afternoon meeting with one of your co-workers, Mary, but she canceled it. You are walking in the hallway when another co-worker also working on the project asks you to give a message to Mary when you see her this afternoon. You cannot deliver the message because you will not be seeing Mary.

You say:

Situation 21: You are shopping in a department store. You have selected an item and are waiting to pay for it. The salesclerk helps you and explains that there is a special offer on a new product and offers to show you a short demonstration. You cannot watch the demonstration because you are on your way to meet someone for lunch.

You say:

Situation 22: You rent a room in a large house. The person who holds the lease lives in the house as well. You are responsible for mowing the lawn every week, a job that takes you about two hours to do. You want the lease-holder to mow the lawn for you this week because you are going out of town. You are in the living room when the lease-holder walks in.

You say:

Situation 23: You are an office manager and are hiring to fill a position that has just opened up. Yesterday, many people filled out application forms for the job. The form is very long and takes most people many hours to complete. You are getting ready to interview an applicant, but cannot find the completed application in the files. You want the applicant to resubmit the application. The applicant is here now for the interview.

You say:

Situation 24: You work as a sales clerk in a department store. A customer is paying for an item and should get three dollars back in change. The customer asks that the three dollars be given in quarters, not dollar bills. You cannot give the change because you do not have enough quarters to spare.

You say:

University of Hawai'i at Manoa
National Foreign Language
Resource Center

Form B

Name: _____   Age: _____

Native language: _____   Sex: _____

Years of English study: _____

Directions: You will hear descriptions of 24 different
situations. Each situation will be repeated once. After the
repetition, say what you would say if you were in the situation
described.

Example:

*Situation: You live in a large apartment building. You are
leaving to go to work. On your way out, you meet your next door
neighbor, whom you haven't seen for a long time.*

[repetition of situation]

You say:

Situation 1: You work in a small department of a large office.
You have worked here for a number of years and are the head of
the department. You are in the office of another member of the
department in a meeting. You accidentally knock over a framed
picture on the desk. It doesn't break.

You say:

Situation 2: You are applying for a job in a company. You go
into the office to turn in your application form to the
manager. You talk to the manager for a few minutes. When you
move to give the manager your form, you accidentally knock over
a vase on the desk and spill water over a pile of papers.

You say:

Situation 3: You are applying for a student loan at a small
bank. You are now meeting with the loan officer. The loan
officer is the only person who reviews the applications at this

bank. The loan officer tells you that there are many other applicants and that it should take two weeks to review your application. However, you want the loan to be processed as soon as possible in order to pay your tuition by the deadline.

You say:

Situation 4: You work for a large company. You and a few of your co-workers are working on a special project. You are just finishing a meeting with the group. The leader of the project asks you to give a message to your secretary. You cannot deliver the message because you are going directly to a meeting scheduled at one of the branch offices.

You say:

Situation 5: You are a member of the local chapter of a national ski club. Every month the club goes on a ski trip. You are in a meeting with the club president, helping plan this month's trip. You want to borrow some paper in order to take some notes.

You say:

Situation 6: You are shopping in a store that sells handmade crafts. You have shopped here a number of times before and usually make a substantial purchase. Today you are looking for a present for your mother's birthday. You are browsing near a clerk. You pick up a small statuette to get a better look at it and drop it on the floor. It breaks.

You say:

Situation 7: You rent a room in a large house. The person who holds the lease lives in the house as well. Each person in the house is responsible for a few hours of chores every week. Your chore is to vacuum the house. This morning when you were using the lease-holder's vacuum you accidentally dropped it and now it does not work. You are now in the living room and the lease-holder walks in.

You say:

Situation 8: You are on an airplane. It is dinner time. The flight attendant sets your food on your tray. You need a napkin.

You say:

Situation 9: You work in a small department of a large office. You have worked here for a number of years and are the head of the department. You have an important meeting scheduled with another member of your department this afternoon. You are in your office when the member stops in and asks to cancel the meeting in order to work on a special project that is due tomorrow. You cannot schedule the meeting for later because you have to report the information to others at a meeting tomorrow.

You say:

Situation 10: Last week you had trouble with your company car and took it to a company mechanic. The mechanic promised to have it ready tomorrow morning. You are going on a business trip tomorrow afternoon and need the car. You stop by the repair shop to make sure the repairs will be finished in time. Now the mechanic tells you the shop is very busy and asks if you can wait an extra day for your car. You cannot delay your trip.

You say:

Situation 11: You are in the airport going through customs after a trip to a foreign country. It is your turn, but when the customs officer asks you for your papers, you realize you do not know where they are. You look in your bag for a little while, find them, and give them to the waiting officer.

You say:

Situation 12: You work in a restaurant. You have just taken a customer's order and are ready to leave the table. The customer is still holding the menu and you need it for another table.

You say:

Situation 13: You are the president of the local chapter of a national camping club. Every month the club goes on a camping trip and you are responsible for organizing it. Last week you were supposed to meet with another member of the club to plan this month's trip. You had to reschedule because you were too busy. The rescheduled meeting was for 7:30 this morning, but you got caught in heavy traffic and just now arrive at the club headquarters. It is 9:00 a.m.

You say:

Situation 14: You live in a large house. You hold the lease to the house and rent out the other rooms. The washing machine is broken. It is Saturday and the repair person is scheduled to fix it this morning. However, you will not be home because you have to pick up your parents at the airport. You want one of your house-mates to stay home this morning. You are in the kitchen when a house-mate walks in.

You say:

Situation 15: You work in a small printing shop. It is late afternoon and a valued customer comes in to ask if you can print 1500 copies of a new advertisement by tomorrow morning. To do this you would have to work into the night. You are tired after a long day and cannot stay late.

You say:

Situation 16: You work in a small department of a large office. You have worked here for a number of years and are the head of the department. You are in a meeting with the other members of your department. You need to write some notes, but realize you do not have any paper. You turn to the person sitting next to you.

You say:

Situation 17: You are a member of the local chapter of a national camping club. Every month the club goes on a camping trip. The president of the club is responsible for organizing the trips, a job that takes a number of hours. You are on this month's trip talking to the president of the club. The president is going to be out of town for a week and asks you to plan the next trip. You cannot plan the trip because you are going to be very busy with work.

You say:

Situation 18: You are in a small family-owned restaurant. You go up to the counter to pay your bill. When you reach to hand your check to the restaurant worker you accidentally knock a few of the menus on the floor.

You say:

Situation 19: You teach in a small school. You have a meeting with the lead teacher for your grade at two o'clock today. When you show up at the meeting it is a few minutes after two.

You say:

Situation 20: You live in a large house. You hold the lease to the house and rent out the other rooms. You are in the living room when one of your house-mates asks to talk to you. Your house-mate explains that it will only take a few minutes and is not important. However, you cannot talk now because you are on your way out.

You say:

Situation 21: You are on your lunch hour. You go into a small shop to look for a present. You find something you like and buy it. As you are ready to leave the clerk explains that the store would like to learn more about it's customers and asks if you would fill out a short questionnaire . You cannot fill out the form because you have to hurry back to work.

You say:

Situation 22: You work for a small department in a large office. The assistant manager of the office gave you a packet of materials to summarize for tomorrow. However, when you start working on the assignment, you realize that you do not have all of the information. You know that the head of the department has the information. You need to get the information, but you know it will take the head of your department about an hour and a half to locate it. You see the head of the department.

You say:

Situation 23: You are the personnel officer in an office that is now hiring new employees. The application form is quite long and takes most applicants several hours to complete. The form must be typed. An applicant comes in and gives you a completed form. However, it has been typed with a very faint ribbon. The application needs to be retyped.

You say:

Situation 24: You work in a small store. A customer comes into the store and asks for change for a ten dollar bill. You cannot give the change because you don't have it in the register.

You say:

University of Hawai'i at Manoa
National Foreign Language
Resource Center

Directions: You will hear descriptions of 24 different situations. Each situation will be repeated once. After the repetition, say what you would say if you were in the situation described.

Example:

Situation: You live in a large apartment building. You are leaving to go to work. On your way out, you meet your next door neighbor, whom you haven't seen for a long time.

[repetition of situation]

You say:

Situation 1: You live in a large house. You hold the lease to the house and rent out the other rooms. You and one of your house-mates had planned to meet at 6:00 this evening to talk about something having to do with the house. However, you were late leaving work. It is a few minutes after 6:00 and as you enter the house you see your house-mate waiting in the living room.

You say:

Situation 2: You are a professional photographer. Last month you took many pictures at a company party. You promised that the prints would be ready for the next company newsletter. The editor of the newsletter comes into your office to pick up the prints, but they are not ready now.

You say:

Situation 3: You have recently moved to a new city and are looking for an apartment to rent. You are looking at a place now. You like it a lot. The landlord explains that you seem like a good person for the apartment, but that there are a few more people who are interested. The landlord says that you will be called next week and told if you have the place. However, you need the landlord to tell you within the next three days.

You say:

Situation 4: You are a member of the local chapter of a national hiking club. You are on a hike now. You and a few other hikers have just stopped for a rest. The president of the club sits next to you, takes out a bottle of water to share with everyone. The president offers the bottle to you first. You have brought your own water.

You say:

Situation 5: You are a member of the local chapter of a national ski club. You are on the club bus and have just arrived at the mountain. You are sitting near the club president. You see that the president is applying sun screen lotion. You want to use the president's lotion because you have forgotten to bring your own. You turn to the club president.

You say:

Situation 6: You are in a computer store sitting at the desk of a salesperson. You have decided to buy several computers for your business and are handing the payment to the salesperson when you accidentally knock over a cup of coffee on the desk. The coffee spills across the desk and onto the salesperson.

You say:

Situation 7: You are a member of a local charitable organization. Last week you promised the president of the organization that you would borrow your friend's truck to help move furniture from one office to the another today. However, you found out this morning that you cannot borrow the truck. You are now at the office and see the president.

You say:

Situation 8: You are shopping in the drug store. You need to buy some envelopes, but cannot find them. You see a salesclerk nearby.

You say:

Situation 9: You live in a large house. You hold the lease to the house and rent out the other rooms. You are talking with one of your house-mates who mentions that this Saturday is a friend's birthday and that plans have been made to have a party at your house. You cannot allow a party next weekend because you have already scheduled for painters to come and paint the inside of the house that same weekend.

You say:

Situation 10: You have organized a good-bye party for a co-worker. Everyone in the office has contributed money to have a photograph of all of the office workers framed. The frame store promised that it would be ready today. You go into the store and the clerk tells you that they are very busy now and asks if you can wait another day. You cannot wait because the good-bye party is this evening.

You say:

Situation 11: You are applying for a loan at a small bank. You have filled out all of the forms and are reaching over the desk to hand them to the loan officer when you accidentally knock over the loan officer's desk calendar.

You say:

Situation 12: You are a salesperson in a gift shop. You need to get something out of a display case now. However, you are unable to get into the case because a customer is standing in the way and blocking your path.

You say:

Situation 13: You work in a small department of a large office. You have worked there for a number of years and are the head of the department. Last weekend you borrowed a co-worker's portable computer because you had a lot of extra work to do and were going out of town. However, you accidentally erased some important information that was stored on the computer. It is Monday morning and you see your co-worker.

You say:

Situation 14: You live in a large house. You hold the lease to the house and rent out the other rooms. Next weekend you are going to put new carpeting in all of the bedrooms. Thus, all of the furniture needs to be moved out of your house-mate's

bedroom next weekend. You are sitting in the kitchen when your
house-mate enters the room.

You say:

Situation 15: You are applying for a job in a large company.
You have just finished an interview with the manager. The
interview went well but took much longer than you expected. You
are getting ready to leave the office when the manager explains
that it is time for a long tour of the company. You cannot go
on the tour because you have another meeting scheduled.

You say:

Situation 16: You and a few of your co-workers are working on a
special project. You have been appointed the project leader.
You are working on the project now and are making a few copies
on the photocopier. One of your co-workers on the project
enters the room. You need a paper clip. You notice that your
co-worker has a box of paper clips.

You say:

Situation 17: You rent a room in a large house. The person who
holds the lease lives in the house as well. Each person in the
house is responsible for a few hours of chores every week. Your
chore is to vacuum the house. The lease holder asks if you can
vacuum the house tomorrow afternoon because visitors are coming
tomorrow night. You cannot vacuum tomorrow afternoon because
you are going to be very busy all day.

You say:

Situation 18: You are buying four tickets to a movie. You have
a coupon for a free ticket. You tell the ticket clerk about the
coupon, but when you look for it you can't find it right away.
After a little while you find the coupon. You hand it to the
clerk.

You say:

Situation 19: You and a few of your co-workers are working on a
special project. You are at a meeting in the office of the
project leader. As you are reaching for your briefcase you
accidentally knock over the project leader's umbrella which was
leaning against the desk.

You say:

Situation 20: You are the president of the local chapter of a national camping club. You are on a camping trip now. One of the club members is putting on mosquito repellent and offers some to you. You do not need to use the repellent because you have your own.

You say:

Situation 21: You are a tourist in a large city. You have taken your film to a photo shop. When you go into the shop to pick up the pictures, the salesperson asks if you would like some coupons for more film developing. You do not need the coupons because you are leaving the city today.

You say:

Situation 22: You work in a small department of a large office. You had an important meeting with the head of your department last week, but you had to cancel it because you got sick. The rescheduled meeting is for this afternoon. You came into the office this morning and felt okay. However, it is now lunch-hour and you are feeling sick again. You want to postpone today's meeting. You go to the office of the department head.

You say:

Situation 23: Last week you had trouble with your company car. You took it to a company mechanic. You need the car tomorrow for an out of town meeting. You go into the shop to pick it up. Now the mechanic says your car will not be ready until this afternoon. However, you have another meeting this afternoon and do not think that you will get out of the meeting until after the shop closes. You want someone to stay late this afternoon in order for you to pick up your car.

You say:

Situation 24: You work as a travel agent in a large department store. You are helping a customer at your desk. The customer gets out a packet of bubble-gum, takes a piece, and offers you a piece. You do not like bubble-gum.

You say:

University of Hawai'i at Manoa
National Foreign Language
Resource Center

Form A

Name: _____   Age: _____

Native language: _____   Sex: _____

Years of English study: _____

Directions: There are 8 roleplays. You will be given a role card before each of the roleplays. The rolecard will describe the situation and your role. If you have questions about the situation or your role, please ask before the roleplay starts. During some of the roleplays, you will be given another role card with further instructions.

Practice Roleplays:

Practice #1 IN YOUR APARTMENT BUILDING

> **Background:** *You live in a large apartment building. You have not seen your neighbor for a long time. You like your neighbor.*
>
> **NOW:** *You are leaving to go to work. On your way out, you meet your next door neighbor.*

Practice #2 AT WORK

> **Background:** *You work in a small company. You are waiting for your co-worker to arrive at a meeting. Last week your co-worker gave a presentation to your department. You think he/she did an excellent job with the presentation. You want to tell your co-worker your opinion about his/her good work.*
>
> **NOW:** *Your co-worker arrives at the meeting.*

Practice #3 AT HOME

Background: *You share a room in a house. Your roommate likes to play loud music in the evenings. You have classes at 7:30 AM every day, so you have to go to bed early. You are finishing some homework and plan to go to bed in a few minutes. Your roommate is not home.*

NOW: *Your roommate walks into the room and turns on the radio.*

#1 AT THE CAR GARAGE

Background 1a: Last week you had trouble with your company van and took it to the company mechanic. The mechanic promised to have it ready by tomorrow at noon. However, you just found out that you have to go on a business trip tomorrow morning and have lots of display materials and samples to bring with you. So, **you need your van to be ready early tomorrow morning.**

NOW: You go into the shop and walk over to the head mechanic who is eating lunch at a work station in the garage.

Background 1b: When the mechanic was gone you accidentally knocked the mechanic's coffee over and it spilled all over some paper work on the table.

NOW: The mechanic comes back.

#2 SHOPPING AT A GIFT SHOP

Background 2a: You have a gift certificate for one of your favorite gift shops. The gift certificate expires next week, but because you are leaving for a three week vacation tomorrow, **you must use the gift certificate today.**

NOW: You are looking at some items in a case. You see something nice, a vase, and **would like to get a better look at it.** The salesclerk walks by.

Background 2b: You decided to buy this item. The salesperson rang up the sale.

NOW: You take out the gift certificate, which you notice is very dirty, and hand it to the salesperson.

#3   AT YOUR HOUSE

Background 3: You live in a large house. You hold the
lease to the house and rent out the other rooms. One of
your house-mates called you at work today (Tuesday) and
said that he/she needed to talk to you about something
having to do with the house. You are happy to meet your
house-mate because you need to talk to your house-mate
about house business too. You and your house-mate decided
to meet at home at 6:00 this evening.

You are working on some home-improvement projects this
month. This coming Saturday afternoon painters are coming
to paint the inside of the house. The painters are very
busy now and you were lucky to be scheduled for this
Saturday. Next Saturday you are going to put new
carpeting in all of the bedrooms. **You need your house-
mate to move all of the furniture out of his/her bedroom
next Saturday so that you can put in the carpeting.**

You were a little late leaving work, so you are a few
minutes late for the meeting.

NOW: You arrive home and see your house-mate waiting in
the living room.

#4   AT WORK BY THE PHOTOCOPIER

Background 4a: You and a few of your co-workers are
working on a special project. You have been appointed the
project leader. You had scheduled a meeting this evening
with one of your co-workers, Mary, but she got sick and
had to cancel the meeting.

You are at the photocopier making a few copies before you
go home for the day (you don't have to stay late since
Mary canceled the meeting). **You need to staple a number
of sets of materials you just copied but you do not have
a stapler with you.**

NOW: One of your co-workers enters the room to ask you
something. You notice that your co-worker has a stapler.

Background 4b: While your co-worker was gone, you
accidentally dropped the stapler on the ground and after
you tried to use it, you realized you broke it. **You want
to tell your co-worker about the stapler when he/she
returns.**

NOW: Your co-worker returns to the room.

#5   APPLYING FOR A NEW JOB

Background 5: You are applying for a new job in a small company and want to make and appointment for an interview. You know the manager, Ms. Kim Green, is very busy and only schedules interviews in the afternoon from one to four o'clock. However, you currently work in the afternoon from noon to five o'clock. **You want to schedule an interview in the morning.**

NOW: Today is Monday. You go into the office at 11:30 in the morning to turn in your application form when you see the manager in the hall.

#6   WORKING AT A JEWELRY REPAIR SHOP

Background 6a: You work in a small shop that repairs jewelry. You do not do the repairs yourself; a repairman comes in at night to do the repairs.

NOW: A valued customer comes into the shop to pick up an antique watch that you know is to be a present. **You need to go in the back room to get the watch, but the customer is standing in the way of the door.**

Background 6b: The repairman has not repaired the watch yet, even though it was supposed to be ready. **You need to tell the customer the watch is not ready yet.**

NOW: Go back out to the customer.

#7   AT WORK AFTER A DEPARTMENT MEETING

Background 7a: You work in a small department of a large office. You have just finished a meeting with the other members of your department. You have to go directly to a meeting at the branch office across town; you will not be going back to your office. The other meeting should last all afternoon. However, before you leave, you need to talk to the head of your department because last week the head of the department loaned you an important book which you have lost. You have already looked everywhere for the book and could not find it. You are certain you have lost the book.

The meeting is over and **you want to tell the head of the department about losing the book before you go the other meeting**.

NOW: The head of the department walks over to you. It looks like he/she wants to tell you something.

Background 7b: You take a look at the materials that the assistant manager compiled. You realize that some of the information is missing. The statistics are not in the materials. You know that the head of the department has the information and that it will take him/her about an hour and a half to locate it. **You need to ask the head of the department for the other information the statistics.**

#8   PHOTOGRAPHY CLUB

Background 8: You are a member of the local chapter of a national photography club. During last month's photography meeting, the club president mentioned that one of his/her cameras needed some repairs. You have a friend who repairs cameras at home for low prices. The president decided to have your friend do the repairs. You have arranged to meet the club president at the club headquarters at five o'clock today to pick up his camera.

You were a little late leaving work, so you are a few minutes late to pick up the camera.

You have also lost the president's phone number, so **you need to ask for it so you can call when the repairs are finished.**

You **need to get home soon** to eat dinner and change your clothes before you have to go back to work in about an hour.

NOW: You arrive and see the president of the club waiting for you.

University of Hawai'i at Manoa National Foreign Language Resource Center

Form A

INTERVIEWER'S GUIDE

Practice Roleplays:

Practice #1 IN YOUR APARTMENT BUILDING

Background: *You live in a large apartment building. You have not seen your neighbor for a long time. You like your neighbor.*

NOW: *You are leaving to go to work. On your way out, you meet your next door neighbor.*

[Interviewer: Replies with standard, friendly answers.]

Practice #2 AT WORK

Background: *You work in a small company. You are waiting for your co-worker to arrive at a meeting. Last week your co-worker gave a presentation to your department. You think he/she did an excellent job with the presentation. You want to tell your co-worker your opinion about his/her good work.*

NOW: *Your co-worker arrives at the meeting.*

[Interviewer: Greetings and thanks for the compliment. Offers a compliment in return on a project.]

Practice #3 AT HOME

Background: *You share a room in a house. Your roommate likes to play loud music in the evenings. You have classes at 7:30 AM every day, so you have to go to bed early. You are finishing some homework and plan to go to bed in a few minutes. Your roommate is not home.*

NOW: *Your roommate walks into the room and turns on the radio.*

[Interviewer: Do not apologize or act sympathetic;
complain that the S goes to bed too early.]

#1   AT THE CAR GARAGE

Background 1a: Last week you had trouble with your
company van and took it to the company mechanic. The
mechanic promised to have it ready by tomorrow at noon.
However, you just found out that you have to go on a
business trip tomorrow morning and have lots of display
materials and samples to bring with you. So, **you need
your van to be ready early tomorrow morning.**

NOW: You go into the shop and walk over to the head
mechanic who is eating lunch at a work station in the
garage.

Background 1b: When the mechanic was gone you
accidentally knocked the mechanic's coffee over and it
spilled all over some paper work on the table.

NOW: The mechanic comes back.

INSTRUCTIONS FOR INTERVIEWER:
- listen to request
- offer a bite to eat
- leave to "ask the other mechanic"
- minimize the offense of the spilt coffee
- tell customer tomorrow morning is fine, van will be
  ready at 7:00 am.

#2   SHOPPING AT A GIFT SHOP

Background 2a: You have a gift certificate for one of
your favorite gift shops. The gift certificate expires
next week, but because you are leaving for a three week
vacation tomorrow, **you must use the gift certificate
today.**

NOW: You are looking at some items in a case. You see
something nice, a vase, and **would like to get a better
look at it.** The salesclerk walks by.

Background 2b: You decided to buy this item. The
salesperson rang up the sale.

NOW: You take out the gift certificate, which you notice
is very dirty, and hand it to the salesperson.

INSTRUCTIONS FOR INTERVIEWER:
- walk by the customer
- take out the vase
- ring up the sale
- accept the certificate
- comment that it is difficult to read
- minimize the offense if customer apologizes
- wrap up the vase
- invite customer to party
- good-byes

#3   *AT YOUR HOUSE*

Background 3: You live in a large house. You hold the lease to the house and rent out the other rooms. One of your house-mates called you at work today (Tuesday) and said that he/she needed to talk to you about something having to do with the house. You are happy to meet your house-mate because you need to talk to your house-mate about house business too. You and your house-mate decided to meet at home at 6:00 this evening.

You are working on some home-improvement projects this month. This coming Saturday afternoon painters are coming to paint the inside of the house. The painters are very busy now and you were lucky to be scheduled for this Saturday. Next Saturday you are going to put new carpeting in all of the bedrooms. **You need your house-mate to move all of the furniture out of his/her bedroom next Saturday so that you can put in the carpeting.**

You were a little late leaving work, so you are a few minutes late for the meeting.

NOW: You arrive home and see your house-mate waiting in the living room.

INSTRUCTIONS FOR INTERVIEWER:
- greet
- minimize the offense of the other being late
- start conversation (may have to jump in and take the floor)
- explain about the party
- listen to other, be pleasant, possibly offer to have party elsewhere
- accept request to move furniture next Sat.
- make positive comment about how nice the house will look

#4   AT WORK BY THE PHOTOCOPIER

Background 4a: You and a few of your co-workers are
working on a special project. You have been appointed the
project leader. You had scheduled a meeting this evening
with one of your co-workers, Mary, but she got sick and
had to cancel the meeting.

You are at the photocopier making a few copies before you
go home for the day (you don't have to stay late since
Mary canceled the meeting). **You need to staple a number
of sets of materials you just copied but you do not have
a stapler with you.**

NOW: One of your co-workers enters the room to ask you
something. You notice that your co-worker has a stapler.

Background 4b: While your co-worker was gone, you
accidentally dropped the stapler on the ground and after
you tried to use it, you realized you broke it. **You want
to tell your co-worker about the stapler when he/she
returns.**

NOW: Your co-worker returns to the room.

INSTRUCTIONS FOR INTERVIEWER:
  • enter room
  • greet other
  • request other to give note to Mary at meeting later
  • accept refusal
  • listen to request to use stapler
  • explain that you need it for a lot of stapling in a
    minute, but that you have to talk to someone so you'll
    be back in a minute
  • listen to apology, milk it if it doesn't seem to be a
    +R
  • good-bye

#5   APPLYING FOR A NEW JOB

Background 5: You are applying for a new job in a small
company and want to make and appointment for an
interview. You know the manager, Ms. Kim Green, is very
busy and only schedules interviews in the afternoon from
one to four o'clock. However, you currently work in the
afternoon from noon to five o'clock. **You want to schedule
an interview in the morning.**

NOW: Today is Monday. You go into the office at 11:30 in the morning to turn in your application form when you see the manager in the hall.

INSTRUCTIONS FOR INTERVIEWER:
- have back to the door
- act startled and drop paper to the floor
- accept/minimize apology
- listen to request
- suggest Thursday morning at 9:00
- request to look at application
- make comments of praise
- recommend that applicant go on a tour before the interview and   suggest now to do it
- accept refusal
- suggest Friday morning for the tour after all
- good-bye

#6   WORKING AT A JEWELRY REPAIR SHOP

Background 6a: You work in a small shop that repairs jewelry. You do not do the repairs yourself; a repairman comes in at night to do the repairs.

NOW: A valued customer comes into the shop to pick up an antique watch that you know is to be a present. **You need to go in the back room to get the watch, but the customer is standing in the way of the door**.

Background 6b: The repairman has not repaired the watch yet, even though it was supposed to be ready. **You need to tell the customer the watch is not ready yet**.

NOW: Go back out to the customer.

INSTRUCTIONS FOR INTERVIEWER:
- stand in front of the backroom door
- request watch and hand over the slip
- move after request to move
- accept that it is not ready, agree to come back tomorrow
- ask for change for the bus
- good-bye, see you tomorrow

Note: Have no change in the till.

#7 AT WORK AFTER A DEPARTMENT MEETING

Background 7a: You work in a small department of a large office. You have just finished a meeting with the other members of your department. You have to go directly to a meeting at the branch office across town; you will not be going back to your office. The other meeting should last all afternoon. However, before you leave, you need to talk to the head of your department because last week the head of the department loaned you an important book which you have lost. You have already looked everywhere for the book and could not find it. You are certain you have lost the book.

The meeting is over and **you want to tell the head of the department about losing the book before you go the other meeting**.

NOW: The head of the department walks over to you. It looks like he/she wants to tell you something.

Background 7b: You take a look at the materials that the assistant manager compiled. You realize that some of the information is missing. The statistics are not in the materials. You know that the head of the department has the information and that it will take him/her about an hour and a half to locate it. **You need to ask the head of the department for the other information the statistics.**

INSTRUCTIONS FOR INTERVIEWER:
- walk over to the co-worker
- ask co-worker to deliver this message to secretary when returns to office now
- ask co-worker to summarize the materials on the Lee account for a meeting tomorrow afternoon, it should take a few hours
- accept the request
- good-bye

#8 PHOTOGRAPHY CLUB

Background 8: You are a member of the local chapter of a national photography club. During last month's photography meeting, the club president mentioned that one of his/her cameras needed some repairs. You have a friend who repairs cameras at home for low prices. The president decided to have your friend do the repairs. You have arranged to meet the club president at the club headquarters at five o'clock today to pick up his camera.

You were a little late leaving work, so you are a few minutes late to pick up the camera.

You have also lost the president's phone number, so **you need to ask for it so you can call when the repairs are finished.**

You **need to get home soon** to eat dinner and change your clothes before you have to go back to work in about an hour.

NOW: You arrive and see the president of the club waiting for you.

INSTRUCTIONS FOR INTERVIEWER:
- greeting
- minimize lateness
- hand over camera
- give phone number
- request that member stay and help you plan next month's trip (you would like member's advice) for about an hour or so
- accept refusal
- good-bye

APPENDIX K: TRAINING MANUAL FOR NATIVE SPEAKER RATERS

OVERVIEW

Your responsibilities will be to rate the appropriateness of NS and NNS responses to DCT items on six aspects: correct speech act, formulaic expressions, amount of speech, and the degree of formality, directness and politeness. Explanations of these aspects, including examples and trouble-shooting, are provided below. An explanation of the criteria for rating follows. The manual concludes with some practice examples.

Your packet contains situations followed by the responses of all subjects to that particular situation. NS and NNS responses have been randomly distributed throughout and are not identified. The responses are numbered and you are to indicate your six ratings of a given response on the Rating Sheet provided.

The scale for rating is a five-point scale with 1 equal to very unsatisfactory and 5 equal to completely appropriate.

```
           very    1 — 2 — 3 — 4 — 5    completely
    unsatisfactory                      appropriate
```

When rating the appropriateness of the speech acts and the expressions used in the response, you are to rate using only the five-point scale. When rating the appropriateness of the amount of information given, and the levels of formality, directness, and politeness, you are to rate on the five-point scale and then, in the case of low ratings (1's and 2's), please indicate if you think the response is inappropriate due to a higher or lesser degree of the aspect in question. For example, say you are rating a response and you think it is far too long. Here you would circle 1 (very unsatisfactory) and then the "+" sign to indicate that it is inappropriate because it is too long. Or say you think a response is not quite formal enough. You would circle 2 and then the "−" sign.

EXPLANATIONS OF THE SIX ASPECTS

Ability to use the correct speech act

Each situation was designed to elicit a particular speech act. You are to consider and rate the degree to which each response captures what you consider to be the speech act the situation was intended to elicit. The question to answer is: How appropriate is this speech act for this situation?

Possible problems in rating: As you read the responses, it should become apparent that speech acts are not mutually exclusive. For example, a request might begin with an apology: "I'm sorry, but could you move your car?" This is still a "true" request. As long as the response includes the speech act within it, it should be considered "appropriate" and rated accordingly. It may also be the case that the response given is very indirect or is intended to introduce a topic without actually getting to the point. In these cases, you should still rate the given response on it's appropriateness in the situation.

It is anticipated that ratings of speech acts will be extreme — either 5 or 1. However, you may use the other numbers on the scale if you think they are appropriate (as might be the case with the very indirect or introduction type responses).

Formulaic Expressions

This category includes use of typical speech, gambits, and so on. Non-typical speech might be due to the non-native speaker not knowing a particular American English phrase or due to some type of transfer. Use of non-typical expressions is not uncommon in these responses and it is anticipated that your native speaker intuitions will serve you well in rating them. The question to ask is: How appropriate is the wording/are the expressions?

Ungrammaticality, however, is not an issue for our purposes. For example, both NNS and NS responses contain errors in verb conjugation and article use. Do *not* let those errors influence your ratings.

Possible problems in rating: Although you might find identifying non-typical speech an easy task, assigning a numerical rating might prove difficult. Further complicating the decision is the fact that some responses contain more than one non-typical wording. As with all of the categories, you are judging the acceptability of the response as a whole. You might also be inclined to include ungrammatical responses in your rating of this category. At times, it might be difficult to distinguish between ungrammatical wording and non-typical wording. When in doubt, follow your native speaker intuitions.

Amount of Speech Used and Information Given

Speakers of any language adjust the amount of speech in a given speech act to fit the particular situation. For example, sometimes speakers feel they want to supply a lengthy explanation when making a request. It has been hypothesized that when a non-native speaker uses more speech than the average native speaker, it is due to two possibilities; the non-native speaker might be of a lower proficiency and thus use circumlocution or other less direct strategies, or the non-native speaker might be of a higher proficiency and thus verbose (Wolfson). Of course, non-native speakers of lower proficiency might use very direct and thus shorter-than-the-average-NS utterances, communicating only the most essential information. For example, a refusal might begin with "I can't" without a reason or excuse because the NNS does not have the language to give such an explanation.

It is not implied, however, that all variation in utterance length is due to language proficiency. Of course, there is a degree of individual choice involved in how much one decides to say. The question here is: How appropriate is the amount of speech used/information given?

Possible problems in rating: Deciding how much speech and/or information is appropriate for a given situation might prove difficult, especially because some individual variation is normal. As a guideline, use your native speaker intuition to judge when a response seems particularly abrupt or seems to "ramble" and provide too much unnecessary information.

Degrees of Formality, Directness, and Politeness

These three distinct yet often overlapping elements of speech have caused a great deal of discussion and research (in addition to headaches!) in pragmatics. These elements are reviewed below. While rating each response, you should try to keep these three concepts as distinct in your mind as possible.

The question is: How appropriate are the levels of formality, directness, and politeness?

Possible problems in rating: You might find it awkward or annoying to assign a rating to these three speech act elements because they are not 100 percent exclusive. Nonetheless, your ratings will give the researchers an indication of the role each of these elements plays in the data and will therefore help the researchers decide how they want to deal with these aspects in the future.

Formality: Formality can be expressed through word choice, phrasing, use of titles, and choice of verb forms. Use of colloquial speech can be appropriate in American English when the situation is informal and between friends, family, and co-workers. Yet here, too, a degree of appropriateness can apply. You are the judge.

Directness: Pragmatically defined, most speech is indirect. However, you are to rate the appropriateness of the level of directness found in the responses. Directness can be indicated by verb form or strategy choice. To illustrate, we offer the well-worn example of the couple sitting in the living room having difficulties with direct and indirect request strategies. Person A (stereotypically the wife) says to Person B, "Boy, it's hot in here!" (an indirect form) thinking that Person B will then get up and open the window. However, Person B replies, "Humm, yeah I guess so" and remains seated. The indirect strategy is ineffective, so Person A gets annoyed and now says, "Hey, bozo, open the window!" (direct form). At this point Person B gets annoyed and replies, "Why didn't you just say so in the first place!" Again, use your native speaker intuition to judge the appropriateness of the level of directness used.

Politeness: This concept has many dimensions and has been the topic of many discussions in speech act studies. Politeness includes the aspects of formality and directness, among other things such as politeness markers ("thank you", "please", "if you don't mind", etc.). Due to its many elements, it is impossible to prescribe a formula of politeness for a given situation. For example, native speakers of English might use first names in a job situation, but it is not necessarily inappropriate to use Mr./Ms./Mrs. (surname) on the job. Furthermore, if one usually uses politeness markers in addition to first names in work situations, one might be seen by others as appropriately polite.

CRITERIA FOR RATINGS

In all of your ratings, you are to use your native speaker intuitions and reactions. As someone with a great deal of experience with NNSs, you might be more accepting than other NSs. However, you are not to rate the responses as the all-accepting-and-culturally-sensitive-ESL-teacher. It is assumed that although you might be more accepting of a response than other more linguistically or culturally isolated NSs, you will still *notice* differences in some of the responses. Therefore, focus on what you notice and, using your native speaker intuitions, compare it to what you think the NS norm might be.

When relying on your NS intuitions, it is assumed that you will employ some type of "band of acceptability". For example, you might find that two responses to the same situation have different degrees of formality, but that both seem acceptable. In such a case, you should rate them as you feel is most appropriate.

Do not use what you think you might say as the sole criteria for your ratings. For example, you might be someone who uses humor very often in interacting with strangers. With this in mind you should not rate other responses negatively just because they do not include the humor you would use in the given situation.

While rating, to the best of your ability, judge each response independently of the others. Try not to let the other responses influence your decision of the response in question. This might prove difficult. Try to clear your mind after each response, thus allowing your native speaker intuition a chance to interact with each response without bias from the last one.

THREE SAMPLES

Example One

Situation: You work in a large company. You and a few of your co-workers are working on a special project. You are talking to the project leader and looking at a copy of the project. You are pointing to something in the paper with your pen and accidentally mark the group leader's copy.

You: _____
_____
_____

Responses:

1. Oh, sorry. Want me to use some White-Out on that?
2. Sorry.
3. I'm sorry. This is yours. I have marked on it without notice.
4. Whoops. Sorry about that.
5. I'm sorry. I'm so careless.

Example Two

Situation: You are an officer in a student organization that has grown rapidly. You realize the need for a new financial officer, a job that will involve a lot of work but not much recognition. You know that one member of the organization is studying accounting. You see that member walking by the library.

You: _____
_____
_____

Responses:

6. I wanted to ask you if you're interested in a new financial officer position in the organization. It's a lot of work, I know, but I think you're perfect for that position.
7. Personal-name, I was wondering if you'd be interested in becoming club-name's new financial officer. I know you are good at accounting, and thought I'd ask you first.
8. Would you be willing to serve as dub accountant?

DEVELOPING PROTOTYPIC MEASURES OF CROSS-CULTURAL PRAGMATICS ◆ 167

9. Could you help our organization's new section?

10. I have a favor to ask you. I heard that you are studying accounting and I was just wondering if you can be the new financial officer for our organization. It would help us quite a lot.

Example Three

Situation: You are president of a student organization. You have a meeting scheduled with another member for this afternoon. You are sitting outside of the library when the member comes over and asks to cancel the meeting in order to work on a term paper that is due tomorrow. You cannot schedule the meeting for later because you have to report the information to several professors at a meeting tomorrow.

You: _____
_____
_____

Responses:

11. I know it is very hard, but I need this for tomorrow meeting, so please finish it by tomorrow.

12. I can really sympathize with you, I know the feeling well. However, my meeting with the professors requires the information no later than tomorrow at 10:00 am and I need your data to compile my report. It's very important that I have that information. I need your help on this.

13. I'll have to discuss the project with the boss tomorrow. Could you finish it by tomorrow?

14. Unnn, the problem that I have with that is that I have to report this into several professors tomorrow. Can't we try to squeeze this in?

15. Could you please finish it until tomorrow?

```
          very    1 — 2 — 3 — 4 — 5    completely
    unsatisfactory                     appropriate
```

Situation						

Response # _____			Response # _____		
speech act	1–2–3–4–5		speech act	1–2–3–4–5	
expressions	1–2–3–4–5		expressions	1–2–3–4–5	
amount/info	1–2–3–4–5	– +	amount/info	1–2–3–4–5	– +
formality	1–2–3–4–5	– +	formality	1–2–3–4–5	– +
directness	1–2–3–4–5	– +	directness	1–2–3–4–5	– +
politeness	1–2–3–4–5	– +	politeness	1–2–3–4–5	– +
Response # _____			Response # _____		
speech act	1–2–3–4–5		speech act	1–2–3–4–5	
expressions	1–2–3–4–5		expressions	1–2–3–4–5	
amount/info	1–2–3–4–5	– +	amount/info	1–2–3–4–5	– +
formality	1–2–3–4–5	– +	formality	1–2–3–4–5	– +
directness	1–2–3–4–5	– +	directness	1–2–3–4–5	– +
politeness	1–2–3–4–5	– +	politeness	1–2–3–4–5	– +
Response # _____			Response # _____		
speech act	1–2–3–4–5		speech act	1–2–3–4–5	
expressions	1–2–3–4–5		expressions	1–2–3–4–5	
amount/info	1–2–3–4–5	– +	amount/info	1–2–3–4–5	– +
formality	1–2–3–4–5	– +	formality	1–2–3–4–5	– +
directness	1–2–3–4–5	– +	directness	1–2–3–4–5	– +
politeness	1–2–3–4–5	– +	politeness	1–2–3–4–5	– +
Response # _____			Response # _____		
speech act	1–2–3–4–5		speech act	1–2–3–4–5	
expressions	1–2–3–4–5		expressions	1–2–3–4–5	
amount/info	1–2–3–4–5	– +	amount/info	1–2–3–4–5	– +
formality	1–2–3–4–5	– +	formality	1–2–3–4–5	– +
directness	1–2–3–4–5	– +	directness	1–2–3–4–5	– +
politeness	1–2–3–4–5	– +	politeness	1–2–3–4–5	– +
Response # _____			Response # _____		
speech act	1–2–3–4–5		speech act	1–2–3–4–5	
expressions	1–2–3–4–5		expressions	1–2–3–4–5	
amount/info	1–2–3–4–5	– +	amount/info	1–2–3–4–5	– +
formality	1–2–3–4–5	– +	formality	1–2–3–4–5	– +
directness	1–2–3–4–5	– +	directness	1–2–3–4–5	– +
politeness	1–2–3–4–5	– +	politeness	1–2–3–4–5	– +

University of Hawai'i at Manoa
National Foreign Language
Resource Center

Form A

Name: _____   Age: _____

Native language: _____   Sex: _____

Years of English study: _____

Directions: Read each of the situations on the following pages. It is expected that you would say something in each of the situations. After thinking about what you would say, give yourself a general rating on your ability to speak appropriately in each situation. Circle the corresponding number (1, 2, 3, 4, or 5) on the sheet. For example, if you think what you would say would be completely appropriate [全く適切], you would circle the number 5. If you think it would be very unsatisfactory [非常に不適切], you would circle 1.

While rating yourself consider your general ability to:
- recognize what you should say
- use appropriate expressions
- use the appropriate amount of speech
- use the appropriate levels of politeness, directness, and formality.

Example:

Situation: You live in a large apartment building. You are leaving to go to work. On your way out, you meet your next door neighbor, whom you haven't seen for a long time.

You might think you would say: "Good morning, Bob. How have you been? We haven't talked for weeks!"

In this case you might circle 5.

                  very 1 — 2 — 3 — 4 —⑤ completely
            unsatisfactory   appropriate

Or you might think you would say: "Nice to meet you. Tell me where you are going. I am thinking you are having a good day today. How is your family?"

In this case you might circle 2 because there are some
inappropriate expressions, and too many expressions over all.

very 1 —②— 3 — 4 — 5 completely
unsatisfactory   appropriate

Situation 1: You live in a large house. You hold the lease to
the house and rent out the other rooms. You are in the room of
one of your house-mates collecting the rent. You reach to take
the rent check when you accidentally knock over a small, empty
vase on the desk. It doesn't break.

Rating: I think what I would say in this situation would be

very 1 — 2 — 3 — 4 — 5 completely
unsatisfactory   appropriate

Situation 2: You work in a small shop that repairs jewelry. A
valued customer comes into the shop to pick up an antique watch
that you know is to be a present. It is not ready yet, even
though you promised it would be.

Rating: I think what I would say in this situation would be

very 1 — 2 — 3 — 4 — 5 completely
unsatisfactory   appropriate

Situation 3: You are applying for a new job in a small company
and want to make an appointment for an interview. You know the
manager is very busy and only schedules interviews in the
afternoon from one to four o'clock. However, you currently work
in the afternoon. You want to schedule an interview in the
morning. You go into the office this morning to turn in your
application form when you see the manager.

Rating: I think what I would say in this situation would be

very 1 — 2 — 3 — 4 — 5 completely
unsatisfactory   appropriate

Situation 4: You are a member of the local chapter of a
national ski club. Every month the club goes on a ski trip. You
are in a club meeting now helping to plan this month's trip.
The club president is sitting next to you and asks to borrow a
pen. You cannot lend your pen because you only have one and
need it to take notes yourself.

Rating: I think what I would say in this situation would be

very 1 — 2 — 3 — 4 — 5 completely
unsatisfactory   appropriate

Situation 5: You work in a small department of a large office. You are in a department meeting now. You need to borrow a pen in order to take some notes. The head of your department is sitting next to you and might have an extra pen.

Rating: I think what I would say in this situation would be

                    very   1 — 2 — 3 — 4 — 5   completely
             unsatisfactory   appropriate

Situation 6: You are an office manager and are interviewing to fill a position that is open. You are interviewing someone now. You walk over to the filing cabinet to get the applicant's application when you accidentally step on a small shopping bag belonging to the applicant. You hear a distinct crunching. You are certain you have broken whatever is in the small bag.

Rating: I think what I would say in this situation would be

                    very   1 — 2 — 3 — 4 — 5   completely
             unsatisfactory   appropriate

Situation 7: You work in a small department of a large office. Last week the head of the department loaned you a computer program on disk. You can't find the disk, and think you have lost it. You have just finished a meeting with your department when the head of the department passes near you.

Rating: I think what I would say in this situation would be

                    very   1 — 2 — 3 — 4 — 5   completely
             unsatisfactory   appropriate

Situation 8: You are shopping for your friend's birthday and see something in a display case. You want to look at it more closely. A salesclerk comes over to you.

Rating: I think what I would say in this situation would be

                    very   1 — 2 — 3 — 4 — 5   completely
             unsatisfactory   appropriate

Situation 9: You live in a large house. You hold the lease to the house and rent out the other rooms. Each person in the house is responsible for a few hours of chores every week. One of your house-mates asks if you can do extra chores this week because your house-mate is going out of town. You cannot do your house-mate's chores this week because you are very busy at work this week and do not have any extra time.

Rating: I think what I would say in this situation would be

very   1 — 2 — 3 — 4 — 5   completely
unsatisfactory   appropriate

Situation 10: You are the manager in an office that is now hiring new employees. Last week an applicant came into the office and scheduled an interview for tomorrow. Now, that same person is in the office asking to reschedule the interview because of a family funeral. You cannot reschedule because you are about to leave the country for two weeks, your schedule is completely full, and you need to hire before you leave.

Rating: I think what I would say in this situation would be

very   1 — 2 — 3 — 4 — 5   completely
unsatisfactory   appropriate

Situation 11: You work in a small shop. You are working in the back room when you hear the bell that tells you there is a customer in the front room. You are on the phone making an important business call. You finish the call as quickly as you can and go out to help the waiting customer.

Rating: I think what I would say in this situation would be

very   1 — 2 — 3 — 4 — 5   completely
unsatisfactory   appropriate

Situation 12: You want to apply for a job in a small office. You want to get an application form. You go to the office and see the office manager sitting behind a desk.

Rating: I think what I would say in this situation would be

very   1 — 2 — 3 — 4 — 5   completely
unsatisfactory   appropriate

Situation 13: You are the president of the local chapter of a national hiking club. Every month the club goes on a hiking trip and you are responsible for organizing it. You are on this month's trip and have borrowed another member's hiking book. You are hiking by a river and stop to look at the book. The book slips from your hand, falls in the river and washes away. You hike on to the rest stop where you meet up with the owner of the book.

Rating: I think what I would say in this situation would be

very   1 — 2 — 3 — 4 — 5   completely
unsatisfactory   appropriate

Situation 14: You have worked in a small department of a large office for a number of years and are the head of the department. You have just been given an extra heavy work assignment to do. You know that one of your co-workers in the department is especially skilled in the area of this assignment. However, you also know that this person is very busy. You want your co-worker to help with the assignment. You go to the desk of your co-worker.

Rating: I think what I would say in this situation would be

very   1 — 2 — 3 — 4 — 5   completely
unsatisfactory   appropriate

Situation 15: You work in a repair shop. One of your valued customers comes in with an antique that is to be a present for a fiftieth wedding anniversary. The customer asks that it be repaired for the party tomorrow. You look at the antique and realize that you cannot do the job in one day. It will take you at least two weeks to finish.

Rating: I think what I would say in this situation would be

very   1 — 2 — 3 — 4 — 5   completely
unsatisfactory   appropriate

Situation 16: You are the president of the local chapter of a national book club. The club reads and discusses a new book every month. You are at this month's meeting, talking with a member of the book club. You need to get the phone number of Sue Lee, another member of the club. You think this person has Sue's number.

Rating: I think what I would say in this situation would be

very   1 — 2 — 3 — 4 — 5   completely
unsatisfactory   appropriate

Situation 17: You are a teacher at a large school. You see the lead teacher on campus. The lead teacher asks you to call all of the other teachers tonight and tell them that there will be a meeting tomorrow. You cannot do it because you know that it will take hours and you have friends coming over to your house tonight.

Rating: I think what I would say in this situation would be

very   1 — 2 — 3 — 4 — 5   completely
unsatisfactory   appropriate

Situation 18: You are in a small bank buying traveler's checks. You move to take the checks when you accidentally knock over a small ceramic figure on the clerk's desk. It doesn't break.

Rating: I think what I would say in this situation would be

very   1 — 2 — 3 — 4 — 5   completely
unsatisfactory   appropriate

Situation 19: You work in a bookstore. You are scheduled to start work at noon today. You will take over for your supervisor who is working the morning shift. You go to work and arrive at the bookstore a few minutes after noon. You see your supervisor.

Rating: I think what I would say in this situation would be

very   1 — 2 — 3 — 4 — 5   completely
unsatisfactory   appropriate

Situation 20: You and a few of your co-workers are working on a special project. You have been appointed the project leader. You are walking in the hallway when another co-worker also working on the project asks you to give a message to Mary when you see her at a meeting you and Mary have scheduled this afternoon. You cannot deliver the message because you will not be seeing her. Mary has canceled the meeting.

Rating: I think what I would say in this situation would be

very   1 — 2 — 3 — 4 — 5   completely
unsatisfactory   appropriate

Situation 21: You are walking through a department store. As you walk past a display, a salesclerk asks you to watch a short video demonstration for a new product. You cannot stop because you are on your way to meet someone for lunch.

Rating: I think what I would say in this situation would be

very   1 — 2 — 3 — 4 — 5   completely
unsatisfactory   appropriate

Situation 22: You rent a room in a large house. The person who holds the lease lives in the house as well. You are responsible for mowing the lawn every week, a job that takes you about two hours to do. You want the lease-holder to mow the lawn for you this week because you are going out of town. You are in the living room when the lease-holder walks in.

Rating: I think what I would say in this situation would be

        very   1 — 2 — 3 — 4 — 5   completely
unsatisfactory   appropriate

Situation 23: You are an office manager and are hiring to fill a position that has just opened up. Yesterday, many people filled out application forms for the job. The form is very long and takes most people many hours to complete. You are getting ready to interview an applicant, but cannot find the completed application in the files. You want the applicant to resubmit the application. The applicant is now here for the interview.

Rating: I think what I would say in this situation would be

        very   1 — 2 — 3 — 4 — 5   completely
unsatisfactory   appropriate

Situation 24: You work as a sales clerk in a department store. A customer is paying for an item and should get three dollars back in change. The customer asks that the three dollars be given in quarters, not dollar bills. You cannot give the change because you do not have enough quarters to spare.

Rating: I think what I would say in this situation would be

        very   1 — 2 — 3 — 4 — 5   completely
unsatisfactory   appropriate

University of Hawai'i at Manoa
National Foreign Language
Resource Center

Form B

Name: _____   Age: _____

Native language: _____   Sex: _____

Years of English study: _____

Directions: Read each of the situations on the following pages.
It is expected that you would say something in each of the
situations. After thinking about what you would say, give
yourself a general rating on your ability to speak
appropriately in each situation. Circle the corresponding
number (1, 2, 3, 4, or 5) on the sheet. For example, if you
think what you would say would be completely appropriate
[全く適切], you would circle the number 5. If you think it
would be very unsatisfactory [非常に不適切], you would
circle 1.

While rating yourself consider your general ability to:
 • recognize what you should say
 • use appropriate expressions
 • use the appropriate amount of speech
 • use the appropriate levels of politeness, directness, and
   formality.

Example:

*Situation: You live in a large apartment building. You are
leaving to go to work. On your way out, you meet your next door
neighbor, whom you haven't seen for a long time.*

You might think you would say: "Good morning, Bob. How have you
been? We haven't talked for weeks!"

In this case you might circle 5.

$$\text{very} \quad 1 - 2 - 3 - 4 - \boxed{5} \text{ completely}$$
$$\text{unsatisfactory} \qquad\qquad\qquad \text{appropriate}$$

Or you might think you would say: "Nice to meet you. Tell me
where you are going. I am thinking you are having a good day
today. How is your family?"

In this case you might circle 2 because there are some
inappropriate expressions, and too many expressions over all.

very   1 –(2)– 3 – 4 – 5   completely
unsatisfactory   appropriate

Situation 1: You work in a small department of a large office. You have worked here for a number of years and are the head of the department. You are in the office of another member of the department in a meeting. You accidentally knock over a framed picture on the desk. It doesn't break.

Rating: I think what I would say in this situation would be

very   1 – 2 – 3 – 4 – 5   completely
unsatisfactory   appropriate

Situation 2: You are applying for a job in a company. You go into the office to turn in your application form to the manager. You talk to the manager for a few minutes. When you move to give the manager your form, you accidentally knock over a vase on the desk and spill water over a pile of papers.

Rating: I think what I would say in this situation would be

very   1 – 2 – 3 – 4 – 5   completely
unsatisfactory   appropriate

Situation 3: You are applying for a student loan at a small bank. You are now meeting with the loan officer. The loan officer is the only person who reviews the applications at this bank. The loan officer tells you that there are many other applicants and that it should take two weeks to review your application. However, you want the loan to be processed as soon as possible in order to pay your tuition by the deadline.

Rating: I think what I would say in this situation would be

very   1 – 2 – 3 – 4 – 5   completely
unsatisfactory   appropriate

Situation 4: You work for a large company. You and a few of your co-workers are working on a special project. You are just finishing a meeting with the group. The leader of the project asks you to give a message to your secretary. You cannot deliver the message because you are going directly to a meeting scheduled at one of the branch offices.

Rating: I think what I would say in this situation would be

very   1 – 2 – 3 – 4 – 5   completely
unsatisfactory   appropriate

Situation 5: You are a member of the local chapter of a national ski club. Every month the club goes on a ski trip. You are in a meeting with the club president, helping plan this month's. You want to borrow some paper in order to take some notes.

Rating: I think what I would say in this situation would be

very   1 — 2 — 3 — 4 — 5   completely
unsatisfactory   appropriate

Situation 6: You are shopping in a store that sells handmade crafts. You have shopped here a number of times before and usually make a substantial purchase. Today you are looking for a present for your mother's birthday. You are browsing near a clerk. You pick up a small statuette to get a better look at it and drop it on the floor. It breaks.

Rating: I think what I would say in this situation would be

very   1 — 2 — 3 — 4 — 5   completely
unsatisfactory   appropriate

Situation 7: You rent a room in a large house. The person who holds the lease lives in the house as well. Each person in the house is responsible for a few hours of chores every week. Your chore is to vacuum the house. This morning when you were using the lease-holder's vacuum you accidentally dropped it and now it does not work. You are now in the living room and the lease-holder walks in.

Rating: I think what I would say in this situation would be

very   1 — 2 — 3 — 4 — 5   completely
unsatisfactory   appropriate

Situation 8: You are on an airplane. It is dinner time. The flight attendant sets your food on your tray. You need a napkin.

Rating: I think what I would say in this situation would be

very   1 — 2 — 3 — 4 — 5   completely
unsatisfactory   appropriate

Situation 9: You work in a small department of a large office. You have worked here for a number of years and are the head of the department. You have an important meeting scheduled with another member of your department this afternoon. You are in your office when the member stops in and asks to cancel the meeting in order to work on a special project that is due tomorrow. You cannot schedule the meeting for later because you have to report the information to others at a meeting tomorrow.

Rating: I think what I would say in this situation would be

very   1 — 2 — 3 — 4 — 5   completely
unsatisfactory   appropriate

Situation 10: Last week you had trouble with your company car and took it to a company mechanic. The mechanic promised to have it ready tomorrow morning. You are going on a business trip tomorrow afternoon and need the car. You stop by the repair shop to make sure the repairs will be finished in time. Now the mechanic tells you the shop is very busy and asks if you can wait an extra day for your car. You cannot delay your trip.

Rating: I think what I would say in this situation would be

very   1 — 2 — 3 — 4 — 5   completely
unsatisfactory   appropriate

Situation 11: You are in the airport going through customs after a trip to a foreign country. It is your turn, but when the customs officer asks you for your papers, you realize you do not know where they are. You look in your bag for a little while, find them, and give them to the waiting officer.

Rating: I think what I would say in this situation would be

very   1 — 2 — 3 — 4 — 5   completely
unsatisfactory   appropriate

Situation 12: You work in a restaurant. You have just taken a customer's order and are ready to leave the table. The customer is still holding the menu and you need it for another table.

Rating: I think what I would say in this situation would be

very   1 — 2 — 3 — 4 — 5   completely
unsatisfactory   appropriate

Situation 13: You are the president of the local chapter of a national camping club. Every month the club goes on a camping trip and you are responsible for organizing it. Last week you were supposed to meet with another member of the club to plan this month's trip. You had to reschedule because you were too busy. The rescheduled meeting was for 7:30 this morning, but you got caught in heavy traffic and just now arrive at the club headquarters. It is 9:00 a.m.

Rating: I think what I would say in this situation would be

very   1 — 2 — 3 — 4 — 5   completely
unsatisfactory   appropriate

Situation 14: You live in a large house. You hold the lease to the house and rent out the other rooms. The washing machine is broken. It is Saturday and the repair person is scheduled to fix it this morning. However, you will not be home because you have to pick up your parents at the airport. You want one of your house-mates to stay home this morning. You are in the kitchen when a house-mate walks in.

Rating: I think what I would say in this situation would be

very   1 — 2 — 3 — 4 — 5   completely
unsatisfactory   appropriate

Situation 15: You work in a small printing shop. It is late afternoon and a valued customer comes in to ask if you can print 1500 copies of a new advertisement by tomorrow morning. To do this you would have to work into the night. You are tired after a long day and cannot stay late.

Rating: I think what I would say in this situation would be

very   1 — 2 — 3 — 4 — 5   completely
unsatisfactory   appropriate

Situation 16: You work in a small department of a large office. You have worked here for a number of years and are the head of the department. You are in a meeting with the other members of your department. You need to write some notes, but realize you do not have any paper. You turn to the person sitting next to you.

Rating: I think what I would say in this situation would be

very   1 — 2 — 3 — 4 — 5   completely
unsatisfactory   appropriate

Situation 17: You are a member of the local chapter of a national camping club. Every month the club goes on a camping trip. The president of the club is responsible for organizing the trips, a job that takes a number of hours. You are on this month's trip talking to the president of the club. The president is going to be out of town for a week and asks you to plan the next trip. You cannot plan the trip because you are going to be very busy with work.

Rating: I think what I would say in this situation would be

very   1 — 2 — 3 — 4 — 5   completely
unsatisfactory   appropriate

Situation 18: You are in a small family-owned restaurant. You go up to the counter to pay your bill. When you reach to hand your check to the restaurant worker you accidentally knock a few of the menus on the floor.

Rating: I think what I would say in this situation would be

very   1 — 2 — 3 — 4 — 5   completely
unsatisfactory   appropriate

Situation 19: You teach in a small school. You have a meeting with the lead teacher for your grade at two o'clock today. When you show up at the meeting it is a few minutes after two.

Rating: I think what I would say in this situation would be

very   1 — 2 — 3 — 4 — 5   completely
unsatisfactory   appropriate

Situation 20: You live in a large house. You hold the lease to the house and rent out the other rooms. You are in the living room when one of your house-mates asks to talk to you. Your house-mate explains that it will only take a few minutes and is not important. However, you cannot talk now because you are on your way out.

Rating: I think what I would say in this situation would be

very   1 — 2 — 3 — 4 — 5   completely
unsatisfactory   appropriate

Situation 21: You are on your lunch hour. You go into a small shop to look for a present for your friend's birthday. You find something you like and buy it. As you are ready to leave the clerk asks to borrow your pen. You cannot lend your pen because you have to hurry back to work.

Rating: I think what I would say in this situation would be

very   1 — 2 — 3 — 4 — 5   completely
unsatisfactory   appropriate

Situation 22: You work for a small department in a large office. The assistant manager of the office gave you a packet of materials to summarize for tomorrow. However, when you start working on the assignment, you realize that you do not have all of the information. You know that the head of the department has the information. You need to get the information, but you know it will take the head of your department about an hour and a half to locate it. You see the head of the department.

Rating: I think what I would say in this situation would be

very   1 — 2 — 3 — 4 — 5   completely
unsatisfactory   appropriate

Situation 23: You are the personnel officer in an office that is now hiring new employees. The application form is quite long and takes most applicants several hours to complete. The form must be typed. An applicant comes in and gives you a completed form. However, it has been typed with a very faint ribbon. The application needs to be retyped.

Rating: I think what I would say in this situation would be

very   1 — 2 — 3 — 4 — 5   completely
unsatisfactory   appropriate

Situation 24: You work in a small store. A customer comes into the store and asks for change for a ten dollar bill. You cannot give the change because you don't have it in the register.

Rating: I think what I would say in this situation would be

very   1 — 2 — 3 — 4 — 5   completely
unsatisfactory   appropriate

University of Hawai'i at Manoa
National Foreign Language
Resource Center

Name: _____   Age: _____

Native language: _____   Sex: _____

Years of English study: _____

Directions: Read each of the situations on the following pages. It is expected that you would say something in each of the situations. After thinking about what you would say, give yourself a general rating on your ability to speak appropriately in each situation. Circle the corresponding number (1, 2, 3, 4, or 5) on the sheet. For example, if you think what you would say would be completely appropriate [全く適切], you would circle the number 5. If you think it would be very unsatisfactory [非常に不適切], you would circle 1.

While rating yourself consider your general ability to:
- recognize what you should say
- use appropriate expressions
- use the appropriate amount of speech
- use the appropriate levels of politeness, directness, and formality.

Example:

Situation: You live in a large apartment building. You are leaving to go to work. On your way out, you meet your next door neighbor, whom you haven't seen for a long time.

You might think you would say: "Good morning, Bob. How have you been? We haven't talked for weeks!"

In this case you might circle 5.

very   1 — 2 — 3 — 4 —(5) completely
unsatisfactory   appropriate

Or you might think you would say: "Nice to meet you. Tell me where you are going. I am thinking you are having a good day today. How is your family?"

In this case you might circle 2 because there are some inappropriate expressions, and too many expressions over all.

---

very 1 –②– 3 – 4 – 5 completely
unsatisfactory   appropriate

Situation 1: You live in a large house. You hold the lease to the house and rent out the other rooms. You and one of your house-mates had planned to meet at 6:00 this evening to talk about house rules. However, you were late leaving work. It is a few minutes after 6:00 and as you enter the house you see your house-mate waiting in the living room.

Rating: I think what I would say in this situation would be

very 1 – 2 – 3 – 4 – 5 completely
unsatisfactory   appropriate

Situation 2: You are a professional photographer. Last month you took many pictures at a company party. You promised that the prints would be ready for the next company newsletter. The editor of the newsletter comes into your office to pick up the prints, but they are not ready now.

Rating: I think what I would say in this situation would be

very 1 – 2 – 3 – 4 – 5 completely
unsatisfactory   appropriate

Situation 3: You have recently moved to a new city and are looking for an apartment to rent. You are looking at a place now. You like it a lot. The landlord explains that you seem like a good person for the apartment, but that there are a few more people who are interested. The landlord says that you will be called next week and told if you have the place. However, you need the landlord to tell you within the next three days.

Rating: I think what I would say in this situation would be

very 1 – 2 – 3 – 4 – 5 completely
unsatisfactory   appropriate

Situation 4: You are a member of the local chapter of a national hiking club. You are on a hike now. You and a few other hikers have just stopped for a rest. The president of the club sits next to you, takes out a bottle of water to share with everyone. The president offers the bottle to you first. You have brought your own water.

Rating: I think what I would say in this situation would be

very 1 – 2 – 3 – 4 – 5 completely
unsatisfactory   appropriate

Situation 5: You are a member of the local chapter of a national ski club. You are on the club bus and have just arrived at the mountain. You are sitting near the club president. You see that the president is applying sun screen lotion. You want to use the president's lotion because you have forgotten to bring your own. You turn to the club president.

Rating: I think what I would say in this situation would be

very   1 — 2 — 3 — 4 — 5   completely
unsatisfactory   appropriate

Situation 6: You are in a computer store sitting at the desk of a salesperson. You have decided to buy several computers for your business and are handing the payment to the salesperson when you accidentally knock over a cup of coffee on the desk. The coffee spills across the desk and onto the salesperson.

Rating: I think what I would say in this situation would be

very   1 — 2 — 3 — 4 — 5   completely
unsatisfactory   appropriate

Situation 7: You are a member of a local charitable organization. Last week you promised the president of the organization that you would borrow your friend's truck to help move furniture from one office to the another today. However, you found out this morning that you cannot borrow the truck. You are now at the office and see the president.

Rating: I think what I would say in this situation would be

very   1 — 2 — 3 — 4 — 5   completely
unsatisfactory   appropriate

Situation 8: You are shopping in the drug store. You need to buy some envelopes, but cannot find them. You see a salesclerk nearby.

Rating: I think what I would say in this situation would be

very   1 — 2 — 3 — 4 — 5   completely
unsatisfactory   appropriate

Situation 9: You live in a large house. You hold the lease to the house and rent out the other rooms. One of your house-mates is talking with you and mentions that it would be a good idea to have a party next weekend. In fact, your house-mate says that the invitations have already been sent out. You cannot allow a party next weekend because you have already scheduled for painters to come and paint the inside of the house that same weekend.

Rating: I think what I would say in this situation would be

very   1 — 2 — 3 — 4 — 5   completely
unsatisfactory   appropriate

Situation 10: You have organized a good-bye party for a co-worker. Everyone in the office has contributed money to have a photograph of all of the office workers framed. The frame store promised that it would be ready today. You go into the store and the clerk tells you that they are very busy now and asks if you can wait another day. You cannot wait because the good-bye party is this evening.

Rating: I think what I would say in this situation would be

very   1 — 2 — 3 — 4 — 5   completely
unsatisfactory   appropriate

Situation 11: You are applying for a loan at a small bank. You have filled out all of the forms and are reaching over the desk to hand them to the loan officer when you accidentally knock over the loan officer's desk calendar.

Rating: I think what I would say in this situation would be

very   1 — 2 — 3 — 4 — 5   completely
unsatisfactory   appropriate

Situation 12: You are a salesperson in a gift shop. You need to get something out of a display case now. However, you are unable to get into the case because a customer is standing in the way and blocking your path.

Rating: I think what I would say in this situation would be

very   1 — 2 — 3 — 4 — 5   completely
unsatisfactory   appropriate

Situation 13: You work in a small department of a large office. You have worked there for a number of years and are the head of the department. Last weekend you borrowed a co-worker's portable computer because you had a lot of extra work to do and were going out of town. However, you accidentally erased some important information that was stored on the computer. It is Monday morning and you see your co-worker.

Rating: I think what I would say in this situation would be

very   1 — 2 — 3 — 4 — 5   completely
unsatisfactory   appropriate

Situation 14: You live in a large house. You hold the lease to the house and rent out the other rooms. This weekend you are going to put new carpeting in all of the bedrooms. Thus, all of the furniture needs to be moved out of your house-mate's bedroom. You are sitting in the kitchen when your house-mate enters the room.

Rating: I think what I would say in this situation would be

very 1 — 2 — 3 — 4 — 5 completely
unsatisfactory appropriate

Situation 15: You are applying for a job in a large company. You have just finished an interview with the manager and are getting ready to leave the office when the manager explains that it is time for a tour of the company. You cannot go on the tour because you did not know about it and have another meeting scheduled in twenty minutes.

Rating: I think what I would say in this situation would be

very 1 — 2 — 3 — 4 — 5 completely
unsatisfactory appropriate

Situation 16: You and a few of your co-workers are working on a special project. You have been appointed the project leader. You are working on the project now and are making a few copies on the xerox machine. One of your co-workers on the project enters the room. You need a paper clip. You notice that your co-worker has a box of paper clips.

Rating: I think what I would say in this situation would be

very 1 — 2 — 3 — 4 — 5 completely
unsatisfactory appropriate

Situation 17: You rent a room in a large house. The person who holds the lease lives in the house as well. Each person in the house is responsible for a few hours of chores every week. Your chore is to vacuum the house. The lease holder asks if you can vacuum the house tomorrow afternoon because the lease-holder is having visitors tomorrow night. You cannot vacuum tomorrow afternoon because you are going to be very busy all day.

Rating: I think what I would say in this situation would be

very 1 — 2 — 3 — 4 — 5 completely
unsatisfactory appropriate

Situation 18: You are buying four tickets to a movie. You have a coupon for a free ticket. You tell the ticket clerk about the coupon, but when you look for it you can't find it right away. After a little while you find the coupon. You hand it to the clerk.

Rating: I think what I would say in this situation would be

very 1 — 2 — 3 — 4 — 5 completely
unsatisfactory   appropriate

Situation 19: You and a few of your co-workers are working on a special project. You are at a meeting in the office of the project leader. As you are reaching for your briefcase you accidentally knock over the project leader's umbrella which was leaning against the desk.

Rating: I think what I would say in this situation would be

very 1 — 2 — 3 — 4 — 5 completely
unsatisfactory   appropriate

Situation 20: You are the president of the local chapter of a national camping club. You are on a camping trip now. One of the club members is putting on mosquito repellent and offers some to you. You do not need to use the repellent because you have your own.

Rating: I think what I would say in this situation would be

very 1 — 2 — 3 — 4 — 5 completely
unsatisfactory   appropriate

Situation 21: You are a tourist in a large city. You have taken your film to a photo shop. When you go into the shop to pick up the pictures, the salesperson asks if you would like some coupons for more film developing. You do not need the coupons because you are leaving the city today.

Rating: I think what I would say in this situation would be

very 1 — 2 — 3 — 4 — 5 completely
unsatisfactory   appropriate

Situation 22: You work in a small department of a large office. You had an important meeting with the head of your department last week, but you had to cancel it because you got sick. The rescheduled meeting is for this afternoon. You came into the office this morning and felt okay. However, it is now lunch-hour and you are feeling sick again. You want to postpone today's meeting. You go to the office of the department head.

Rating: I think what I would say in this situation would be

very 1 — 2 — 3 — 4 — 5 completely
unsatisfactory   appropriate

Situation 23: Last week you had trouble with your company car. You took it to a company mechanic. You need the car tomorrow for an out of town meeting. It is Monday morning and the mechanic said your car would be ready this afternoon. However, you have another meeting this afternoon and do not think that you will get out of the meeting until after the shop closes. You go to the shop now. You want someone to stay late this afternoon in order for you to pick up your car.

Rating: I think what I would say in this situation would be

very   1 — 2 — 3 — 4 — 5   completely
unsatisfactory   appropriate

Situation 24: You work as a travel agent in a large department store. You are helping a customer at your desk. The customer gets out a packet of bubble-gum, takes a piece, and offers you a piece. You do not like bubble-gum.

Rating: I think what I would say in this situation would be

very   1 — 2 — 3 — 4 — 5   completely
unsatisfactory   appropriate

University of Hawai'i at Manoa
National Foreign Language
Resource Center

Name: _____   Age: _____

Native language: _____   Sex: _____

Years of English study: _____

Directions: Watch the videotape of yourself doing the
roleplays. Each roleplay was designed to include a request, a
refusal, and an apology. Before you watch each roleplay, the
scene will be reviewed and you will be told when you were
supposed to have made the request, refusal, and apology. After
watching the videotape, think about what you said and give
yourself a general rating on your ability to speak
appropriately for the request, the refusal, and the apology.
Circle the corresponding number (1, 2, 3, 4, or 5) on the
sheet. For example, if you think what you would said was
completely appropriate [全く適切], you would circle the
number 5. If you think it would be very unsatisfactory
[非常に不適切], you would circle 1.
    While rating yourself consider your general ability to:

• recognize what you should say
• use appropriate expressions
• use the appropriate amount of speech
• use the appropriate levels of politeness, directness,
  and formality.

Example:

Read the situation, then watch the two different roleplays to
get a better understanding of the rating scale.

*Situation: You live in a large apartment building. You are
leaving to go to work. On your way out, you meet your next door
neighbor, whom you haven't seen for a long time.*

You might think you would say: "Good morning, Bob. How have you
been? We haven't talked for weeks!"

In this case you might circle 5.

                    very   1 — 2 — 3 — 4 —(5) completely
            unsatisfactory   appropriate

Or you might think you would say: "Nice to meet you. Tell me
where you are going. I am thinking you are having a good day
today. How is your family?"

In this case you might circle 2 because there are some
inappropriate expressions, and too many expressions over all.

very 1 — (2) — 3 — 4 — 5 completely
unsatisfactory   appropriate

SELF-ASSESSMENT OF INTERVIEW

<u>Scene One — At the Car Garage</u>
1. Request
>   very   1 — 2 — 3 — 4 — 5   completely
>   unsatisfactory   appropriate

2. Refusal
>   very   1 — 2 — 3 — 4 — 5   completely
>   unsatisfactory   appropriate

3. Apology
>   very   1 — 2 — 3 — 4 — 5   completely
>   unsatisfactory   appropriate

<u>Scene Two — Shopping at a Gift Shop</u>
1. Request
>   very   1 — 2 — 3 — 4 — 5   completely
>   unsatisfactory   appropriate

2. Apology
>   very   1 — 2 — 3 — 4 — 5   completely
>   unsatisfactory   appropriate

3. Refusal
>   very   1 — 2 — 3 — 4 — 5   completely
>   unsatisfactory   appropriate

<u>Scene Three — At Your House</u>
1. Apology
>   very   1 — 2 — 3 — 4 — 5   completely
>   unsatisfactory   appropriate

2. Refusal
>   very   1 — 2 — 3 — 4 — 5   completely
>   unsatisfactory   appropriate

3. Request
>   very   1 — 2 — 3 — 4 — 5   completely
>   unsatisfactory   appropriate

<u>Scene Four — At Work by the Photocopier</u>
1. Refusal
>   very   1 — 2 — 3 — 4 — 5   completely
>   unsatisfactory   appropriate

2. Request
>   very   1 — 2 — 3 — 4 — 5   completely
>   unsatisfactory   appropriate

3. Apology
>   very   1 — 2 — 3 — 4 — 5   completely
>   unsatisfactory   appropriate

Scene Five — Applying for a New Job

1. Apology
                    very   1 — 2 — 3 — 4 — 5   completely
                 unsatisfactory   appropriate

2. Request
                    very   1 — 2 — 3 — 4 — 5   completely
                 unsatisfactory   appropriate

3. Refusal
                    very   1 — 2 — 3 — 4 — 5   completely
                 unsatisfactory   appropriate

Scene Six — Working at a Jewelry Repair Shop

1. Request
                    very   1 — 2 — 3 — 4 — 5   completely
                 unsatisfactory   appropriate

2. Apology
                    very   1 — 2 — 3 — 4 — 5   completely
                 unsatisfactory   appropriate

3. Refusal
                    very   1 — 2 — 3 — 4 — 5   completely
                 unsatisfactory   appropriate

Scene Seven — At Work after a Department Meeting

1. Refusal
                    very   1 — 2 — 3 — 4 — 5   completely
                 unsatisfactory   appropriate

2. Apology
                    very   1 — 2 — 3 — 4 — 5   completely
                 unsatisfactory   appropriate

3. Request
                    very   1 — 2 — 3 — 4 — 5   completely
                 unsatisfactory   appropriate

Scene Eight — Photography Club

1. Apology
                    very   1 — 2 — 3 — 4 — 5   completely
                 unsatisfactory   appropriate

2. Request
                    very   1 — 2 — 3 — 4 — 5   completely
                 unsatisfactory   appropriate

3. Refusal
                    very   1 — 2 — 3 — 4 — 5   completely
                 unsatisfactory   appropriate

CPSIA information can be obtained
at www.ICGtesting.com
Printed in the USA
BVOW06s2132070218
507582BV00001B/39/P